D0789578

AGING AIRCRAFT

USAF Workload and
Material Consumption
Life Cycle Patterns

Raymond A. Pyles

RAND
Project AIR FORCE

Prepared for the United States Air Force

The research reported here was sponsored by the United States Air Force under Contract F49642-01-C-0003. Further information may be obtained from the Strategic Planning Division, Directorate of Plans, Hq USAF.

Library of Congress Cataloging-in-Publication Data

Pyles, Raymond, 1941-
    Aging aircraft : USAF workload and material consumption life cycle patterns /
Raymond A. Pyles.
     p. cm.
    "MR-1641."
    Includes bibliographical references.
    ISBN 0-8330-3349-2 (pbk.)
    1. Airplanes, Military—United States—Maintenance and repair. 2.
United States. Air Force—Ground support. I.Title.

UG1243.P96 2003
358.4'183'0973—dc21

                                  2003005775

Cover design by Barbara Angell Caslon

Published 2003 by RAND
1700 Main Street, P.O. Box 2138, Santa Monica, CA 90407-2138
1200 South Hayes Street, Arlington, VA 22202-5050
201 North Craig Street, Suite 202, Pittsburgh, PA 15213-1516
RAND URL: http://www.rand.org/
To order RAND documents or to obtain additional information,
contact Distribution Services: Telephone: (310) 451-7002;
Fax: (310) 451-6915; Email: order@rand.org

Throughout the 1990s and into this century, the United States Air Force (USAF) has found it necessary to retain its aircraft fleets for unprecedentedly long service lives. Current plans forecast keeping portions of some existing fleets for as long as 80 years of service.

The safety, aircraft availability, and cost implications of that fleet-retention policy are unknown. Project AIR FORCE's Aging Aircraft Project is conducting a wide range of studies to improve the Air Force's ability to foresee those implications and identify actions that will mitigate or avoid some of the more severe consequences.

This study measures how the USAF aircraft fleets' ages relate to maintenance and modification workloads and material consumption. It will provide the foundation for future estimates of the effects of those activities on maintenance-resource requirements, aircraft availability, and annual operating costs. Thus, it should be of interest to force planners, maintenance production planners, maintenance policy analysts, system program directors, and logistics and cost analysts.

Planners can use the empirical and analytic results in this report to forecast how workloads and costs may grow in both the near term and long term. System program directors can use those results to gain an integrated perspective of the end-to-end resource and budget implications for their weapon systems. Logistics and cost analysts should be interested in how this analysis dealt with the wide range of confounding factors that may affect the measurement of age-related workload growth and in the way in which different patterns of growth are exhibited for different aircraft designs for different categories of workloads and material consumption.

PROJECT AIR FORCE

Project AIR FORCE (PAF), a division of RAND, is the Air Force federally funded research and development center (FFRDC) for studies and analyses. It provides the Air Force with independent analyses of policy alternatives affecting the development, employment, combat readiness, and support of current and future aerospace forces. Research is performed in four programs: Aerospace Force Development; Manpower, Personnel, and Training; Resource Management; and Strategy and Doctrine. The research described in this document was performed in the Resource Management Program.

Additional information about PAF is available on our web site at http://www.rand.org/paf.

CONTENTS

FIGURES

TABLES

SUMMARY

The Air Force is now passing through a period of transition. Throughout the Cold War, when the force-structure and force-age profiles were roughly constant, Air Force planners and programmers could rely on the retirement of older aircraft to free up the maintenance funds and capacity for both newer aircraft and the growing demands of the remaining aging fleets. Relying on retirement is no longer a part of current plans for the force structure. Instead, some aircraft fleets will have unprecedentedly long service lives. The straight-lining (i.e., zero-growth forecasting) of maintenance-related budget requirements beyond the next year or two underestimates future maintenance requirements, often substantially. Since the U.S. government uses a 6-year forecast to plan expenditures, those longer-term maintenance-budget shortfalls can be resolved only by reprogramming funds from other initiatives or accepting decreased aircraft availability for operations and training. Near-term budgeteers and programmers need to know the consequences of funding maintenance at various levels in the face of growing workloads.

But funding ever-increasing annual maintenance workloads and material consumption is not the only problem. Maintenance requires both human and material capital, which must be acquired and trained, to develop the maintenance capacity needed for those growing workloads. Facility and equipment upgrades may take two to three years to develop. Once funds are available, hiring a new employee and training him or her to a journeyman skill level takes even longer. Expanding capacity by hiring contractors may take still longer, because contractors face those problems plus a steep learning curve when they accept an unfamiliar workload. Planners of maintenance workload capacity and personnel need to know the approximate sizes of the workloads as much as six to ten years in advance so that they can acquire funds in time to develop sufficient capacity.

Finally, there is the problem of replacing an aircraft fleet because its operating costs or its availability is no longer acceptable. Typical lead times for developing and fielding an initial operating capability for an aircraft design range from ten to 15 years. Once an initial operating capability has been fielded, it may take ten to 20 more years to replace a large fleet at modern production rates. Air Force force-structure planners need to know when total operating costs or fleet availability will reach unacceptable levels.

The analysis reported here proposes models for forecasting age-related maintenance and modification workload and material consumption patterns to aid capacity, funding, and force-structure planners develop cost-effective, realistic plans to sustain older fleets while evaluating cost-effective fleet-replacement plans.

ANALYTIC APPROACH

Two conceptual models of workload and material consumption growth over aircraft service lives were posited, one for maintenance, another for modification. The models build on previous research into age-related maintenance and modification workload growth. Both conceptual models allowed for both growth and decline at different ages, but the modification model allowed for episodic surges when major modifications were required.

In contrast to the approaches in many previous studies, the analytic approach used here sought to distinguish long-term age-related growth from other life-cycle events that may obscure or exaggerate measured workload growth. For example, during a platform's early life, "infantile" failures caused by design or manufacturing errors and initial "honeymoon" periods, when many aircraft components have not yet begun to fail, may change workloads dramatically, but they may have little relationship to the cumulative effects of material degradation as a platform enters its second and higher decade of service. Alternatively, exogenous events, such as changes in accounting systems, how the force is organized, size or posture of the wing or maintenance organization, skill levels, or maintenance procedures, may also affect workloads and hide or exaggerate the apparent effects of age.

In addition, most previous studies based their forecasts of future workloads on either linear- or compound-growth equations. Over the long periods now envisioned for retaining Air Force aircraft, the two equations yield substantially different forecasts. Compound equations imply continuously accelerating exponential workload growth; the linear equation implies more-modest, constant growth. Thus, it is important to test for the presence of acceleration in order to forecast workloads far into the future.

To complicate the forecasting issue still further, the maintenance conceptual model forecasts that, as a direct consequence of the design-life limits introduced by the original design and manufacturing processes, total workloads and material consumption must ultimately decelerate. If so, early- and mid-life growth may overestimate later-life growth. Again, we need to test the available historical data for that possibility in order to forecast far into the future. Thus, the study used regression analysis to address five questions:

1. Do older fleets experience higher maintenance or modification workloads and material costs?

2. If workloads and costs are higher, how rapidly do they grow with age?

3. Do different platforms experience different rates of growth?

4. Do different maintenance activities experience different growth patterns?

5. What are the prospects for continued growth? Will the growth accelerate, decelerate, or remain the same?

The answers should make it possible to improve forecasts of future maintenance and modification workloads and material consumption, and their associated costs. To answer the questions, we examined life-cycle patterns for the following workload and cost-growth categories:

- Base-level on-equipment (mostly flightline) maintenance

- Base-level off-equipment (mostly component repair) maintenance
- Base-level periodic aircraft inspections
- Base-level special inspections
- Base-level demands for depot-level reparable component repairs (DLR repairs)
- Base-level consumption of General Stock Division (GSD) material
- Base-level replacement of support equipment
- Planned programmed depot maintenance (PDM) of aircraft
- Planned depot engine overhaul
- Contractor logistics support (CLS), priced on an annual per-aircraft basis
- CLS priced on a per-flying-hour basis
- Depot-level modifications installed as part of a Time-Change Technical Order (TCTO)
- DLR replacement and modernization.

Data were not available to examine life-cycle workload and cost patterns for the following:

- Unscheduled depot-level maintenance (UDLM; sometimes called speedline maintenance), in which unexpected repairs are made to damaged aircraft
- Over-and-above depot-level maintenance, in which defects discovered during PDMs are repaired
- Modification-kit design and fabricate costs
- Software maintenance.

Multiple regression analyses were conducted for each workload and material consumption category in turn, using available historical data for multiple United States Air Force (USAF) aircraft. Depending on the available data, control variables were entered for aircraft fly-away cost, calendar year, major operating command, basic aircraft mission (e.g., fighter, bomber, cargo), several break-in periods (e.g., infantile-failure or honeymoon periods), in addition to the aircraft age and an age–flyaway cost interaction term. For engine workloads, engine weight was used instead of flyaway cost. We used a stepwise approach to eliminate statistically nonsignificant terms and so that a simple linear relationship that retained any significant terms could be identified.

A post-hoc test was then performed to detect any acceleration or deceleration. It added a second-order term centered on age 20 years. That age was chosen to minimize any correlation between the linear and second-order terms. If the second-order term was statistically significant, acceleration (or deceleration) had been detected in that workload or material consumption category.

Statistical tests (Cook's distance and leverage) were also performed to detect the presence of any data points that might have an undue influence on the resulting equations. When those tests indicated some possibility of undue influence, we removed the offending points so that we could observe the effects on the stepwise regression reductions. When those results yielded a substantially different relationship, both results were reported and the implications discussed.

LATE-LIFE GROWTH FINDINGS[1]

Maintenance workloads and material consumption generally exhibited late-life growth as aircraft aged, but the rate of that growth depended on both the aircraft's flyaway cost and the workload category. Long-term, late-life growth was found in all base-level and depot-level maintenance workloads and material consumption categories except base-level periodic inspections, per-flying-hour contractor logistics support, and depot modification workloads.

Often, growth rates depended on the aircraft flyaway costs: More-expensive aircraft experienced higher growth rates. Of course, growth rates in engine overhaul workload depended not on aircraft

---

[1]See Chapter Five, "Summary of Findings" and "Summary of Major Age-Related Findings" sections and Tables 5.42 and 5.43.

flyaway cost but on engine weight: Heavier engines exhibited higher rates of growth.

Little evidence was found for the accelerating growth implicit in the compound-growth equations. The only exceptions were PDM workloads, for which a second-order term centered on age 20 was significant. This finding indicates that PDM workload growth does accelerate, at least through the 40 years of experience available to date.

Except for General Support Division (GSD) consumable materials, no workload or material consumption category exhibited any late-life deceleration. Even the GSD result may be illusory. The available GSD data end about the age of the peak consumption. Thus the second-order deceleration may only reflect a prolonged honeymoon period for some long-lived consumable parts.

Finally, depot-level aircraft modernization workloads (TCTO workloads) exhibited a statistically significant surge during the period between 20 and 25 years of age. This surge may reflect the limits of the designers' ability to forecast operational performance requirements. As a result, the Air Force may find it necessary to reinvest periodically to keep retained aging platforms operationally viable as operating environments evolve.

OTHER WORKLOAD AND COST FINDINGS

Where data were available, all workload and cost categories were affected by differences across Major Operating Commands (MAJCOMs; e.g., Air Combat Command, Air Mobility Command) and early-life honeymoon or infantile-failure periods.

Such early-life transitions pose an especially difficult problem for those who would predict later-life growth. This analysis found both honeymoon and infantile-failure patterns, depending on the workload category. Honeymoon effects' low initial workloads would cause later-life growth rates to be overestimated; infantile failures would cause such rates to be underestimated. In either case, forecasters of late-life workloads can improve their forecasts by discounting such early-life transitions. (See Chapter Five "Findings for On-Equipment (Flightline) Workloads" section for an example of both infantile failures and a honeymoon period.)

The causes of differences in base-maintenance workloads across MAJCOMs cannot be determined from these data. While some of those differences may reflect variations in operating environments or maintenance philosophies, they may also reflect different reporting practices. In any case, the large differences found in this study may hide or exaggerate the effects of age in other studies, if the MAJ-COMs' fleets have different ages. (See Chapter Five "Findings for On-Equipment Workloads" for an example of differences between commands.)

IMPLICATIONS FOR PLANNING[2]

Obviously, the growth rates and life-cycle workload patterns reported here can be translated into estimates of future aircraft availability and cost, based on the planned evolution of the USAF force structure. Work is under way to develop a long-term forecasting tool suitable for future maintenance and modification costs for alternative force-structure plans. Computational approaches are also being developed to forecast aircraft availability from aggregate maintenance or workload data. Those improved forecasts are an essential element for planning during the period of transition to an older force through which the Air Force is now passing.

IMPLICATIONS FOR MAINTENANCE POLICIES AND PRACTICES[3]

Despite the analytic results reported here that should improve workload and cost forecasts, considerable uncertainty remains about how future maintenance and modification workloads may grow. First, some statistical uncertainties are inherent in the forecasting equations developed in this study. The size of those uncertainties generally grows as one extrapolates beyond the ages at which the Air Force has operated aircraft. This study estimates the size of those

---

[2]See Chapter Six, "Six Strategies" section.

[3]See Chapter Six, "Facing Demand and Supply Uncertainties" section.

uncertainties for each workload or material consumption category. Perhaps more important, the study identifies a number of factors (new material deterioration processes and natural limits to workload growth) that could emerge as those fleets age further. Those factors represent nonstatistical (sometimes called structural) uncertainties that, if they emerge, could dwarf the statistical uncertainties. In light of those uncertainties, the Air Force needs to adopt a twin policy of

- improving its understanding of the causes of workload changes

- reducing its susceptibility to unexpected changes.

Age does not directly cause the measured workload patterns. It is only a correlate of many other material-deterioration and maintenance-response processes that change over time. The Air Force might be able to mitigate the workload growth if it better understood the underlying causes and potential remedies.

That improved understanding will take time to develop. Until the causes and remedies are better understood, the Air Force will need to hedge against those uncertainties. Such hedging strategies might include contingency plans for replacing older fleets, maintaining several fleets with overlapping capabilities to minimize the risk of early retirement, or developing spare maintenance capacity to ensure against the effects of unexpected maintenance workload growth for older fleets.

ACKNOWLEDGMENTS

Many people contributed to the substance of this report. Most important, I would like to thank Brig Gen James Totsch, who first raised the issue of whether fleet aging might be an important contributor to the growth in aircraft maintenance workload and cost that the Air Force experienced in the late 1990s. Other Air Force personnel who provided substantive insights about aircraft life-cycle patterns and other chronological events that influenced this study's findings include Col William Foulois, Col Tommy Hixon, Col Joanne Rodefer, Col Frederick Jones, Lt Col John Orsato, Lt Col Carl Rehberg, Lt Col Larry Butkus, Maj Dale Colter, Maj Kenneth Sebek, and Donald Pearce. This work also benefited substantially from receiving programmed depot maintenance workload historical data from the B-52, C-5, C-130, C-135, C-141, and F-15 Program Offices.

Several contractor personnel have also been unstinting in their support, providing both data and insights about material-degradation effects. I would like to thank Michael DiDonato and Kenneth Sperry of Boeing, along with Allan Haenish of ANSER Corporation.

Several RAND colleagues sharpened my thinking and analysis. Laura Baldwin, Jean Gebman, Tim Ramey, and Hy Shulman each contributed ideas and concepts that refined the research objectives, approach, and interpretation of the results. Greg Hildebrandt and Man-Bing Sze provided the residual analysis and prediction-error analysis. The technical reviewers, Lionel Galway and Elvira Loredo, suggested several ways to improve the technical foundation of the key points. Bob Roll, whose Resource Management Program supported the work, provided both solid encouragement and critical commentary throughout the study. Finally, Marian Branch greatly improved the presentation and clarity of this report through her editorial skills and determination.

Chapter One

INTRODUCTION

As it enters the twenty-first century, the United States Air Force (USAF) faces three challenges in its quest to maintain a highly capable, state-of-the art force: increased aircraft unit costs, reduced military budgets, and the continued need for a force structure sufficient to meet the nation's worldwide commitments.

After a nearly 40-percent force reduction in the early 1990s, the Air Force has maintained a total force of about 6,300 aircraft to meet current military force-structure goals. If the service wished to modernize its fleet by replacing each aircraft every 20 years, as it did in the 1970s, it would need to acquire about 315 aircraft per year. Unfortunately, the unit cost of modern aircraft has increased substantially since then. For example, a KC-135 tanker built in the 1950s–1960s cost about $40 million in today's dollars (U.S. Air Force, AFCAIG, 1998c), whereas a 767-400ER–based replacement aircraft would cost about $125 million for the unmodified airframe alone (Boeing Corporation, 2001).

In addition, the Air Force's total budget has declined in real terms, a decline made possible by reductions in total force size and in the number of bases. However, it has proven exceedingly difficult to reduce Operations and Maintenance (O&M) and Personnel budgets in proportion to the force structure. Whereas Research, Development, and Testing and Procurement budgets constituted about half the total Air Force budgets in the 1980s, they are now less than a third (Mehuron, 1992–2001).

As a consequence of rising unit costs and declining budgets during the decade of the 1990s, the Air Force had found it necessary to slow the rate at which it replaced older aircraft. In the 1980s, the service was able to acquire an average of about 270 aircraft per year ("Fixed-Wing Aircraft Trends," 2001); in 2001, it acquired just 63 aircraft (excluding civil air patrol aircraft) (U.S. Air Force, 2000).

Such a reduction obviously reduces annual procurement expenses; however, it requires that the Air Force retain at least some of its fleets for a longer time. At the rate of just 63 aircraft per year, the Air Force would need about 100 years to replace every aircraft in its current fleet just once. Although current plans call for increasing aircraft procurement rates over the next several years, the planned rates do not approach historical levels.

The consequences of depending on aging fleets may include higher flight-safety risks, reduced aircraft availability and readiness, and higher maintenance and modification costs. Aviation engineers and managers have become so concerned about potential age-related flight-safety issues caused by material deterioration that they have initiated a new series of worldwide conferences (Conference on Aging Aircraft sponsored by Galaxy Scientific Corporation, Egg Harbor Township, New Jersey). For its part, the USAF found it necessary at various times in the 1990s to restrict some C-5, C-141, and KC-135 flight operations temporarily to deal with age-related flight-safety surprises.

Aging fleets' material deterioration and the remediation of emerging flight-safety problems may also require increased maintenance and modification times, which would reduce the number of Air Force aircraft available for military operations and training. In addition, senior USAF officials have frequently cited fleet ages as one of several factors that may cause decreased readiness (Ryan, 1999; Roche, 2002).

Older fleets may also need higher annual sustainment budgets. Some observers speculate that increased material degradation will require steadily increasing resources and costs for maintenance labor and material. Others suggest that the Air Force may need to increase modification budgets substantially to acquire operational capabilities in the aging fleets that would have been incorporated in new replacement aircraft as a matter of course.

In their most extreme versions, these concerns have caused some observers to raise the specter of a death spiral (Gansler, 1999) or train wreck (Goure and Ranney, 1999) in procurement spending, because Operations and Support expenditures may require an increasingly larger share of future annual Air Force budgets. Those observers worry that age-driven O&S cost increases may force reductions in procurements, which may further increase fleet ages, in turn forcing still further reductions in procurements, thus creating a self-destructive downward spiral in modernization.

SCOPE OF THIS STUDY

This study sought to provide the empirical foundations for forecasting aircraft availability and costs. Assuming that the Air Force would continue its long tradition of responding rapidly when flight safety or mission capability fall into jeopardy, the study measured how aircraft maintenance and modification workloads and material consumption have historically grown as aircraft age, and it identified implications for future workload growth. Specifically, it addressed five questions:

1. Do older fleets experience higher maintenance or modification workloads and material costs?

2. If workloads and costs are higher, how rapidly do they grow with age?

3. Do different platforms experience different rates of growth?

4. Do different maintenance activities experience different growth patterns?

5. What are the prospects for continued workload growth? Will growth accelerate, decelerate, or remain the same?

The study did not examine how the maintenance and modification workloads and material consumption of other Air Force major end items (e.g., ground support equipment, munitions, missiles, and ground radars) may grow with age. It also did not examine the secondary implications of maintenance growth on indirect base operating support requirements (such as vehicle maintenance, medical support, and housing). Parameters were developed for equations to predict future workloads and costs from fleets' ages and other factors.

Future studies will apply these equations to estimate how that workload growth may affect future aircraft availability and annual Air Force budgets, and to evaluate the economic consequences of alternative fleet recapitalization plans. Other analyses are under way to address similar age-related maintenance-cost growth experienced by commercial airlines, and to discuss the potential implications of age-related material degradation for flight safety.

ORGANIZATION OF THIS REPORT

This report summarizes previous research on aging aircraft and reports our analytic approach and findings. The above five questions provide a framework for each chapter. Chapter Two begins with a brief overview of previous research. Chapter Three relates that research to the underlying effects of material degradation, operational demand evolution, and technology progress. Chapter Four discusses the analytic framework, data sources, and approach. Chapter Five reports where growth in maintenance and modification workload and material consumption was found. Chapter Six draws some initial implications for USAF action.

Chapter Two

PREVIOUS RESEARCH ON THE RELATIONSHIP BETWEEN AGE AND MAINTENANCE WORKLOADS OR COST

Despite the recognition of age as a potential cause of increased work-loads and maintenance costs as early as the 1960s, analysts have addressed the problem only sporadically until the 1990s. The recent increase has been enabled by larger volumes of longitudinal data and more-sophisticated analytic techniques, but it has been motivated by an increasing concern that aging fleets' costs may increase substantially and rapidly. Most early efforts examined depot costs for aircraft overhauls, engine overhaul, or aircraft component repair in isolation. Recent analyses have sought a more comprehensive view.

SUMMARY OF THIS CHAPTER

Limited historical data, imprecise and unstable accounting practices, and changing incentives have limited analysts' ability to measure relationships between aircraft age and maintenance workloads or total operating cost. More-recent studies have had better access to longitudinal data. Even so, both cost analyses and workload analyses in the 1990s had been confounded by process changes, incentive changes, and accounting aggregation and allocation practices that obscured the effects of age on workloads and costs.

Previous studies of growth in Air Force aircraft maintenance and modification workload have been particularly constrained by limited longitudinal data. Even in this study, some workload data were available only for selected aircraft and for limited periods. In future years, the advent of new, long-term maintenance data-collection, storage, and retrieval systems will facilitate more-effective, comprehensive analyses, particularly the Core Automated Maintenance System and Reliability and Equipment Management Information System for USAF base-level workloads and the Weapon System Cost Recovery System (WSCRS) and the Programmed Depot Maintenance Support System (PDMSS) for depot workloads.

Nevertheless, some analyses of USAF workload and cost data have exploited the available data to the extent possible. USAF, Boeing, the Congressional Budget Office (CBO), and RAND analysts found relatively large annual growth in KC-135 Programmed Depot Maintenance (PDM) workloads (10 percent, linear), base-level engine repair workloads (5.3 percent, compound), depot-level engine overhaul workloads (4.5 percent, compound), and overall O&M and O&S costs (3 percent and 1 percent, compound, respectively).

Using the U.S. Navy's 20-year repository of depot and base maintenance data, Navy analysts found a wide range of fighter and helicopter flightline workload growth (between 1.9 and 7.9 percent annually, depending on the platform), and moderately high growth for intermediate (mostly component) repair (4.7 percent annually), depot aircraft maintenance (6.0 percent), and depot engine overhauls (6.6 percent). Using more aggregated data, CBO analysts found overall Navy aircraft O&S costs increased 1 percent annually.

Few empirical studies of commercial airline experience have been published. None has estimated annual workload or cost-growth rates, but Boeing analysts (Boeing Corporation, 2001) report nominal late-life growth in heavy-maintenance costs for selected Boeing and McDonnell-Douglas passenger aircraft. Perhaps more important, they also report observing a consistent early-life "honeymoon" period, a period as long as 5–10 years during which heavy-maintenance costs are low. By contrast, the general reliability literature cites a bathtub curve, which indicates an early-life downward-sliding ramp of declining infantile failures over the same period as design and manufacturing errors are corrected. One interpretation of the different observations may be that different workloads experience early-life transition patterns that differ from others. Thus, some workloads may exhibit patterns that are different from others as aircraft age through their life cycle.

Those studies raise as many issues as they resolve. Most report finding growth in workload or cost, but they also found wide growth-rate variations across individual platform designs, and wide variations in growth depending on the work location (flightline, intermediate, or depot) and on work content (components, engines, or aircraft inspections). None examined material costs or modifications independently.

More seriously for the purposes of forecasting USAF workloads and costs, these studies did not consider the issues associated with generalizing beyond the range of available data. If we wish to forecast total USAF workloads and costs, we must also perform forecasts for aircraft just entering the inventory or still on the drawing boards. Thus, we must forecast not only how today's fleets' workloads or costs will grow but also how those other fleets' costs will vary. For example, most analyses did not address the issue of honeymoon or break-in periods and how they might exaggerate or hide later-life growth when included in an analysis. No analyses considered how the linear and compound forms diverge when extrapolated; consequently, they did not test the relative validity of alternative forms. Finally, the aggregated analyses did not consider how much the aggregated forecast may underestimate future costs if only one cost element grows rapidly at a compound rate.

AVAILABILITY OF WORKLOAD AND COST DATA HAMPERED MOST EARLY STUDIES

Early analysts concerned with estimating Operations and Support (O&S) costs were able to gather only limited data to examine age-related maintenance and modification effects. For example, Marks and Hess (1981) identified age as an important potential cause of increased depot maintenance and modification workloads, but they eliminated age in their analysis for lack of sufficient longitudinal data. In particular, they could not determine to what extent workload differences were due to improved design or manufacturing processes instead of to age.

Mixing up design maturity and age can create a problem, as demonstrated in a 1962 RAND study by Johnson, who found a very strong negative relationship between aircraft age and the 1961 depot maintenance workloads. Like Marks and Hess two decades later, Johnson had no longitudinal data and only a limited pool of 1961 depot maintenance data for individual aircraft designs. Thus, his analysis spanned the range from the Century Series (F-100 to F-106) and C-135 variants (fielded in the 1950s) back to the C-47 and C-54 (fielded in the 1930s). Of course, the 1940s and 1950s saw great advances in aircraft design sophistication—for example, jet engines, aluminum airframes, and increasingly sophisticated onboard avionics. Much of Johnson's negative relationship between age and depot-support cost may have reflected workload increases caused by the massive increase in aircraft complexity and capabilities over that period; age-related maintenance growth may have been obscured.

The earliest attempt to discriminate the effects of design from age appeared in Nelson's (1977) analysis of USAF aircraft engine workloads, which found that average depot-level aircraft engine maintenance costs rose 4.5 percent annually and base-level costs rose 5.3 percent annually. Although he also had only one year's data for a dozen engines, Nelson used the engine-production cost (adjusted for inflation) and a design-aggressiveness variable (that measured how early or late a particular engine type-model-series (TMS) design achieved performance characteristics compared to a derived state-of-the-art measure) to measure the potential effects of technology improvements in more-modern designs. He also found that more-expensive engines were more costly to support, as were engines whose designs pushed the state of the art more aggressively.

Nelson's 1977 study faced many challenges, including an exceptionally small sample (12 data points), no data for the new modular fighter engines, and no data about on-condition engine maintenance processes just being introduced. (*On-condition maintenance* is a process that streamlines maintenance to replace only components whose condition had reached unacceptable limits, rather than replace all the wear-prone parts.) Thus, a forecaster could not be confident about extrapolating his findings to more-modern engines being maintained under revised maintenance policies. Even this study was hampered by the lack of data covering a wide range of engine designs and maintenance policies.

Nelson's study also identified one important variable whose presence makes it difficult to estimate the overall age effects: engine-overhaul interval. Nelson found that the per-overhaul costs diminish time between overhauls as the time between overhauls increases, and that base-level maintenance workloads decrease even more rapidly as that interval increases. That non-intuitive result (accumulated work decreases if the period for accumulating it increases) arises from the engineers' conservatism regarding the early-life reliability of the engine. As Nelson describes, engineers' confidence in the engine reliability grows as modifications are introduced to remedy early reliability problems. As their confidence grows, the engineers increase the interval between overhauls. Thus, the interval is increased when the engineers are confident that recent modifications have made the engine more reliable. A more reliable engine will probably require less maintenance work when it is overhauled, so the (more-reliable) engines have both longer service between overhauls and less work per overhaul. That age-dependent interval-extension process would counteract the effects of the pure age variable. Thus, Nelson's age-related workload-growth rates may overstate the effects of age on total base and depot maintenance costs, because the age-related effects of any overhaul-interval extension are not included directly.

Recent Studies Have More Data, but Cost Analyses Have Been Confounded by Accounting Practices and Changing Organizations

Beginning in the early 1960s, the USAF has invested progressively more resources in collecting and maintaining information about its maintenance and support operations and costs. More-recent studies have benefited greatly from being able to draw on a comprehensive body of cost, engineering, and operational historical data. The USAF, of course, was not alone in this effort. Other military departments, civil aviation agencies (particularly the Federal Aviation Administration), airlines, and aircraft manufacturers also began to collect and use more time-series databases about the evolving costs and effects of aircraft maintenance.

Accounting Practices Confound Age Effects on Measured Mission Design Series Costs. Hildebrandt and Sze (1990) were among the first to exploit the increased availability of even limited USAF longitudinal data. They found a 1.7-percent age-related annual relationship between total O&S costs of USAF aircraft and fleet ages, based on USAF cost data from 1981 through 1986. As with prior studies, their analysis relied mainly on measured differences in costs across different mission designs (MD), due to the short historical period available for study.

When Hildebrandt and Sze eliminated the contributions of fuel and personnel costs, their 1.7-percent relationship eroded to only a 0.5-percent annual increase. Thus, much of the overall measured effect could be attributed to the introduction of more fuel-efficient engine designs and personnel management initiatives, not to the aging of the fleets themselves.

In a more recent attempt to examine the effects of aircraft age on total O&S costs, Kiley (2001) repeated the Hildebrandt and Sze analysis with more-recent, but also more-aggregated, data for O&S budgets for both USAF and Navy aircraft. He found that the O&S portion of USAF and Navy aircraft–related budgets increased 1 to 3 percent for each additional year of aircraft age.

Total-Cost Analyses May Obscure Underlying Maintenance Workload Growth. The weak relationships found in both the Hildebrandt and Sze and the Kiley studies may be a product of the data they had available and the inclusion of support costs that may not change as aircraft age. Limitations in their cost data made it necessary for both studies to use an age variable that averaged fleet ages across all variants—called mission design series, or MDS—of a basic mission design. That is, F-15As and F-16As delivered during the 1970s were treated as though they had the same age as F-15Cs and F-16Cs delivered in the 1980s or 1990s. Likewise, C-5As were assumed to be the same age as C-5Bs produced 16 years later.

In addition, the analyses were limited by the lack of actual cost data. USAF bases require large amounts of resources that are shared by collocated units and aircraft, including the following:

•   Non-maintenance unit-level personnel

•   Installation support and indirect personnel

•   Unit-level material consumption other than petroleum, oil, and lubricants (POL) and training ordnance

- Over half of the on-equipment depot maintenance
- Most of the depot component repair
- The depot material management, contracting, and other administrative functions.

To relate the costs of the resources to the aircraft consuming them, the USAF allocates their total costs to individual MDS fleets. Age was not included as a factor in those after-the-fact cost allocations, because the relationships have never been established. It is hard to imagine how either study could have detected any age-related effects when a large fraction of the costs are allocated artificially. More important, including these six costs may have caused the two analyses to underestimate the size of the actual growth by adding noise that enhanced the tendency of statistical regressions to underestimate relationships in the presence of noisy data.

Budgets Respond Slowly to Workload Shifts. In addition, the military services' expenditures in specific budget elements tend to mute the effects of workload changes, reallocating personnel and other resources from underutilized workloads to overloaded areas. Even when total workloads ebb and flow over time, personnel managers hesitate to respond too quickly, because the effect may be temporary. The costs and disruption associated with acquiring and training a skilled workforce combine with the inevitable workload fluctuations to make personnel managers reluctant to increase or decrease the workforce with every change in workload levels.

Resource Levels Often Do Not Reflect Workload Shifts. The costs of USAF aerospace maintenance personnel are particularly insensitive to age-related changes in workload, because their numbers are based on assessments of likely wartime workloads. Thus, even fairly sizable peacetime workload growth may have only modest effects on the costs of peacetime military maintenance personnel—until some critical threshold at which units have insufficient personnel to meet the wartime workloads is passed.

Taken together, accounting cost allocation practices, budget sluggishness, and relatively fixed aerospace-maintenance-personnel requirements dampen some effects of age on measured costs when Air Force total-cost histories are examined.

SOME STUDIES HAVE FOCUSED MORE HEAVILY ON WORKLOAD DATA

In efforts to see behind the total-cost data, some analysts have shifted their attention to direct measures of maintenance workloads. Because those workloads are generally measured at different centers and in different data systems, the studies may lack the grand scope of the total-cost analyses. However, they avoid many of the measurement problems of those aggregate analyses. Thus, the workload-based analyses often report substantially larger growth rates. More important, they recognize that workloads' life-cycle patterns may differ, so it becomes possible to identify which additional resources may be needed.

In addition, at least some workload data files have higher quality and coverage than the cost data, depending on the reporting and archiving procedures in force at different locations. Many maintenance data systems report actual work hours spent by aircraft tail number (which can be related to both age and MDS), rather than planned or budgeted manhours paid.

As important, some maintenance data systems have been in operation for several decades, providing a much longer longitudinal track than cost data. For example, the Navy maintenance data system has been in operation for over 20 years at shipboard and continental United States (CONUS) base and depot locations; therefore, naval logistics analysts have been able to collect the kind of longitudinal data needed to detect and measure growth in age-related maintenance workloads at those locations for their aircraft. Likewise, the Air Force's Maintenance Data Collection (MDC) system has been used for many years at base level to collect data for analyzing base-level operations and to support maintenance manpower planning since the 1960s. Over the years, the USAF has developed a Core Automated Maintenance System (CAMS) that has improved base flightline and intermediate data-entry accuracy and, more recently, a Reliability, Equipment and Maintainability Information System (REMIS) that archives the CAMS data over many years. Unfortunately, no formal recording and archiving process is in place for the Air Force depots' actual work performed on a per-aircraft basis; actual longitudinal depot-workload data exist for only a few depot activities.

Implicitly, previous studies have placed maintenance workloads into several different categories according to aircraft platform, workload content, and workload location, considering one aircraft mission design or mission design series at a time, focusing on one kind of work (e.g., on-aircraft, on-engine, or component repair), and examining one echelon (base, shipboard, or depot) at a time. Even those studies that examined multiple workloads usually analyzed them separately, estimating growth for one kind of work performed on one MDS at a particular echelon. The following discussion organizes previous research along similar lines, discussing base and depot workload growth for each of three work-content categories: on-aircraft, on-engine, and component repair.

On-Aircraft Workload Studies Consistently Found Growth at Base and Depot

Past studies of workload growth found that both technology and maintenance posturing decisions may cause different workloads to experience different growth rates. Thus, different aircraft may experience different growth rates for the same technology, and different technologies on the same aircraft may experience different maintenance growth. Further, workload at different echelons may experience different growth rates. This subsection summarizes workload growth findings from the base-level studies first, then discusses the depot workload studies.

Base-Level On-Equipment Workload Analyses Consistently Found Age-Related Growth. We found no analyses of age-related growth in base-level on-aircraft workload for Air Force aircraft, but we located three studies of Navy shipboard and base-level on-aircraft workload growth, which should be similar in kind and amounts to Air Force aircraft.

Using data covering the period from 1979 through 1992, Johnson (1993) found a systematic increase in reported total (i.e., on-aircraft and intermediate combined) maintenance manhours per flying hour for five Navy aircraft (F-14, F/A-18, H-53E, E-2C, and C-2A), ranging from 2.4 percent annually (for older C-2As) to 7.9 percent (for H-53Es). Moreover, he was able to relate a substantial portion of the workload increase to an increase in the frequency of demands, after controlling for operational tempo (OPTEMPO). He also noted in passing that the workload for some F/A-18 subsystems, particularly power plant (engine), flight control, and various electrical and electronic subsystems, seemed to grow faster than that for others.

Stoll and Davis (1993) examined 1983–1992 field-level on-aircraft maintenance workloads for ten Navy aircraft (P-3C, S-3A, CH-53E, SH-60B, SH-3E, CH-46E, E-2C, A-6E, F-14A, and F/A-18A) and found lower growth rates than Johnson did for unit-level on-aircraft maintenance workload growth after controlling for OPTEMPO: from 1.4 to 5.4 percent. They also found a small difference between fixed-wing and helicopter on-equipment workload growth (4.0 percent versus 3.4 percent). As discussed below, they also found somewhat larger growth rates in intermediate maintenance.

Finally, in a detailed multiple regression analysis of F/A-18C historical monthly workloads by aircraft tail number from 1990 through 1999, Francis and Shaw (2000) found annual growth rates in total squadron-level workloads of 6.5 to 8.9 percent. They also found a seasonal effect (December exhibiting lower workloads), a flying-hour effect (especially for deployed sorties), and a Marine effect (the Marines reported lower workloads than did Navy units). Most interestingly, they found a strong (over 6-percent) relationship between age and maintenance workload in an analysis of a 1996 subset of the data, dispelling any notion that the growth may be caused by changes in system processes over time. They also found that older aircraft failed more often after a carrier sortie: The probability of those aircraft requiring unscheduled maintenance rose 0.8 percent for each year of age. (That is, a 10-year-old aircraft would fail 8.2 percent more often after a carrier sortie than would a brand-new one.)

Depot-Level On-Equipment Workload Analyses Also Consistently Found Growth. Ad hoc Air Force data-retention policy for depot on-aircraft maintenance has limited analysts' ability to estimate general trends across multiple aircraft types. Only one aircraft, the KC-135, had more than ten sequential years of historical data.

However, that aircraft's programmed depot maintenance workload has been analyzed extensively. Ramsey, French, and Sperry (1998) reported a linear (simple) annual growth rate of 10 percent in KC-135 core PDM workload over the 1988–1998 period. (When measured as a compound annual rate over ten years, this value is equivalent to 6.9 percent annually.) When new, one-time tasks, such as rewiring the aircraft, were included, they found a 13-percent annual linear growth rate (8.3 percent, compound). In a separate paper, Sperry (1998) compared the KC-135 growth rates to those of commercial aircraft heavy maintenance reported by DiDonato and Sweers (1997): 6.4, 5.2, and 5.9 percent (linear) for the 747-200, the 727-200, and the 737-200, respectively.

DiDonato and Sweers (1997) also reported observing low initial levels of maintenance workloads in early life, calling the initial low-maintenance period a honeymoon, which suggests a period when maintenance workloads remain low for some time. Of course, their observations contrast with the general reliability literature that reports an initial period with a high failure rate for new equipment as design errors and manufacturing flaws are gradually identified and resolved.

A recent analysis of the KC-135 economic service life (KC-135 ESL) (KC-135 ESL Integrated Product Team, 2001) constructed a forecast based on both historical workload trends and engineering estimates or future required repairs. That forecast estimated a 6-percent linear annual PDM cost growth rate for the next 40 years of KC-135 operation.

The KC-135 ESL also examined the relationship between cumulative aircraft exposure to corrosive environments and the number of major structural repairs (MSRs) required during PDMs. While MSRs constitute a small workload by themselves, they can cause a long delay during PDMs because other PDM work must be suspended when major structural elements are removed for refurbishment. The analysis was much more complicated than described here; however, the forecast MSR growth rate was equivalent to 0.7 percent annually.

Working with direct maintenance labor, overhead, and direct material consumption data, Stoll and Davis (1993) also examined Navy scheduled depot-level maintenance (SDLM). They found an average 6-percent annual increase in on-aircraft maintenance costs, after controlling for OPTEMPO and inflation. Their estimate also compensated for an accounting shift during the period, whereby direct material costs increased substantially due to a process and accounting change that eliminated government-furnished material.

On-Engine Overhaul Workloads Grow as Engines Age

Engines and engine modules are different from most components, because their logistics-support policies involve a periodic remanufacturing or overhaul of serial-number–controlled engines or engine modules to a like-new condition. In the overhaul, each engine is removed from the fleet when it approaches a theoretical life limit determined by the material characteristics of several components. At that time, the engines are disassembled, inspected for defects, and reassembled from existing, new, and remanufactured components, as needed. Engine or module components judged to be fully serviceable through the next overhaul are retained, but all other components are replaced.

An engine's service life between overhauls is shorter than an aircraft's design service life (e.g., 6,000 tactical cycles, or about 2,400 flying hours, versus 8,000 flying hours for an F-16 aircraft). Therefore, an engine may undergo several overhauls within the service life of the aircraft on which it was originally installed. Thus, the logistics system might overhaul a typical fighter engine to almost like-new condition every six to 12 years, depending on the flying program. Many components are new, although some (those with longer intrinsic lives) will be removed during a later overhaul cycle. Because most of the new components will also require replacement at the same time, the workload and material consumption increase with each sequential overhaul.

Some observers may imagine that this continual renewal process might hold back the onslaught of age-related material degradation in engine support. Nelson did not find that to be the case in his 1977 report on engine life-cycle costs. Instead, he found that both base and depot repair costs tend to increase with age (5.3 and 4.5 percent, respectively), despite periodic engine remanufacture during the overhaul process.

Stoll and Davis (1993) found slightly higher growth for Navy depot-level fixed-wing engine rework (6.6 percent annually). Simpler helicopter engines grew at only 2.2 percent annually. Stoll and Davis did not report unit-level on-engine maintenance growth rates.

In their review of TF33-P102 (KC-135E) engines, the KC-135 ESL study (2000) found an annual linear growth of 3.75 percent in total engine removal (TER) rate since 1985 and an annual linear growth rate in single overhaul costs of 45 percent in overhaul costs since 1995. Much of the explosive overhaul cost growth in that period was attributed to accounting changes (including the discontinuance of job routing, whereby engine components were sent to other shops and only repair costs were incurred as a direct labor charge); therefore, the ESL team used only the earlier pre–accounting-change data (1990–1997) and estimated an overhaul cost growth of 2.25 percent. The joint effect of a 3.75-percent TER growth and a 2.25-percent overhaul cost growth would be a 6.1-percent annual linear workload growth rate.

In their study of the F108 (KC-135R) engine, the KC-135 ESL study found that TER was actually decreasing because of the engine's youth. The study then used engineers' experience with other commercial engines to estimate that the F108 TER would grow 6 percent annually. As with the TF33, the F108 engine overhaul costs rose dramatically (an average of 12 percent linear per year) during the 1997–2000 period due to accounting changes. But unlike the TF33, the 1990–1997 costs per overhaul had declined steadily prior to 1997, so the study team estimated a linear growth rate of 3 percent annually in the future. Again, combining the TER and the per-overhaul cost growth would be equivalent to a linear workload growth rate of over 9 percent.

Few Analyses Have Addressed Aging Components

Aircraft subsystems, such as flight controls, electrical systems, and hydraulics, are subject to the same kinds of material degradation as aircraft structures, deteriorating over time from the combined effects of corrosion and fatigue.

Other material-degradation processes may also be at work. For example, in the 1980s the F-16 low-power radio frequency (LPRF) unit experienced rapidly deteriorating performance caused by slow, age-related migration of iridium atoms in the solder to the gold connector pins, where they formed a barrier to the radio-frequency signals essential to the LPRF's function. Designers and logisticians alike were surprised when the failure rate suddenly climbed and the repair success rate declined. Other, more mundane examples of nonstructural material-degradation processes abound, including embrittlement of wire casings, delamination of composite materials, and the cumulative effects of dirt and grit in electronics and control systems.

We found only one previous analysis that addressed age-related effects on base-level component repair workloads. Stoll and Davis (1993) found that growth in intermediate maintenance workload (mostly component repair) slightly exceeded Navy on-aircraft maintenance workload growth for fixed-wing aircraft (4.7 percent versus 4.0 percent). In contrast, they found helicopter intermediate maintenance grew at 12.4 percent annually (compared with 3.4 percent for on-helicopter workload growth). They reported that the higher helicopter workload growth may be spurious, because, during the analysis period, intermediate maintenance responsibility for the SH-60B and the CH-53E had shifted from interim contractor support to organic repair.

Material Consumption May Increase with Workload

Whether replacing a failed component on an avionics box, retreading a tire, or replating a strut, most maintenance processes consume not only labor but also material. If technicians must respond more frequently to breaks or if their work requires fixing more subsystems or components, they may consume more material in the process. Indeed, the Air Force Material Command (AFMC) implicitly takes this position in its pricing, because it computes an average cost per depot product standard hour (DPSH), which includes an average cost for material.

Most Air Force research has found no evidence of a relationship between age and material costs, partly because, as described earlier in this chapter, the Air Force's cost-accounting processes do not trace material usage to a specific aircraft or the fleet to which that aircraft belongs. Because so many data are averaged across fleets of varying ages, there is no completely accurate way to estimate how aircraft or component age might affect material consumption.

For example, a C-5A and a C-5B would appear to have exactly the same material-consumption rates for every component they share, even though the C-5A is 16 years older than the C-5B. Such identical rates would be accurate if both drew from the same pool of spares and if aircraft condition did not affect removals. If degraded wiring or other aircraft-related material degradation affects component removals in older aircraft, current statistics for component removal rate could not capture that effect.

In their analysis of growth in Navy repair parts requirements, Stoll and Davis (1993) distinguished between consumable materials and depot-level reparable (DLR) spare parts. (DLRs are usually expensive, complex parts that can be repaired at depots. Consumable parts are usually simpler and cheaper to replace than to repair.) They found mixed evidence that consumable-material consumption increased with aircraft age (again, controlled for OPTEMPO). In particular, they found that both the budgets and reported supply costs for consumables declined during the analysis period, but that the reported consumables usage from unit-level maintenance reporting systems increased. They could not ascertain whether these inconsistencies were due to a drawdown of supply material over time, a change in maintenance material usage reporting, or some other factor. For their part, the authors reported their belief that, because the maintenance data do reflect actual maintenance-action–generated consumable usage, they should be considered more representative of the underlying trends than the flight-hour program [budget]-related data.

They found a similar inconsistency when they compared total DLR replacement costs (including supply system overhead) and depot component-repair costs from 1985 through 1991. While total supply system costs decreased 5.8 percent annually from 1986 to 1991, depot maintenance costs (direct labor and material per flying hour) increased about 25 percent per year between 1988 and 1991. The apparent inconsistency may reflect a unit-level behavior similar to that observed when the Air Force instituted a similar change in the funding of DLR support. In the Air Force, units began consolidating broken subcomponents into higher-level assemblies, reducing the number of broken components being sent to the depots (at a previously agreed price) while increasing the complexity (and cost) of the repair actually required (Camm and Shulman, 1993).

Ratliff and Tiller (1999) examined the cost growth for Navy aviation DLRs between 1988 and 1996. They found no general relationship between aircraft average age and DLR consumption per flying hour. Their analysis used MDS average age and workload per flying hour, with no control for the relative MDS complexity or initial reliability. In addition, they note that Navy aircraft have parts of differing ages (just as do Air Force aircraft), so maintenance growth caused by older parts may be obscured by modifications, purchases of individual components, or the general movement of components across aircraft.

Modification Age-Related Cost Patterns Have Not Been Analyzed

To our knowledge, there have been no previous studies of growth in age-related modification cost. In the past, it may have been irrelevant, because only a few aircraft platforms were retained long enough to require upgrading to meet more-modern operating requirements. As likely, the data for such analyses have been difficult to obtain.

ASSESSMENT OF PREVIOUS RESEARCH

One view of the previous research is that it has laid a substantial foundation for understanding how maintenance workloads and material costs have evolved as past fleets have aged over their service lives. With only one or two exceptions, the analysts found that maintenance workloads (or costs) grew. Some analysts have observed that the workloads may not grow at a constant rate over time. Others have measured different growth rates for different workloads, different platform types (rotary versus fixed-wing), or different aircraft designs. Some found modest overall cost growth in aggregate operating costs; others found somewhat larger growth in individual workloads. Some have noted the importance of controlling for other exogenous effects, such as organizational differences or changes in internal processes, to avoid potential mismeasurement of growth rates.

But the challenge facing the Air Force is not to understand how past fleets' maintenance and modification workloads and costs have evolved over past service lives. Instead, it must *forecast* how fleets' workloads, availability, and costs will change when the aircraft in them are kept up to twice as long. Armed with such information, the Air Force could better decide when it would be economically or operationally prudent to replace aircraft, modify them, or make maintenance investments and expenditures.

Of course, the Air Force would not need long-term forecasts if it could acquire new aircraft quickly. Initiatives are under way to shorten acquisition lead times; however, lead times to design and procure the initial operating capability of a new fleet have typically exceeded a decade. Worse, budget constraints rarely allow for rapid wholesale replacement of fleets exceeding one or two dozen aircraft. Thus, the Air Force must make strategic decisions about fleet replacements many years in advance. If maintenance costs or fleet availability will deteriorate unacceptably before a fleet can be replaced, Air Force policymakers and resource managers need to know that with enough lead time to forestall those effects.

Viewed in this light, the previous research raises five issues that must be addressed if future workloads, availability, and costs are to be forecast as the Air Force keeps its fleets for unprecedentedly long service lives:

- Identifying constant versus variable growth patterns
- Using linear versus accelerating growth equations
- Generalizing across fleets
- Controlling for calendar and organizational effects
- Budgeting for modification life cycle patterns.

Once again, the previous research provides insights into these issues. The first three issues are closely related because they identify errors that may arise when a pattern observed in a given period is extrapolated beyond the limits of the available data. The fourth issue recognizes that the effects of some exogenous change can be construed as being caused by aircraft age. The last issue simply seeks to discover any age-related pattern.

Identifying Constant Versus Variable Growth Patterns

DiDonato and Sweers (1997) observed that workloads may grow at non-constant rates as aircraft age. Yet most research to date has assumed that one constant rate was sufficient to characterize a fleet's workload growth. While a constant rate may be adequate for estimating workloads within the range of previous historical data (depending on the accuracy required), it may not be adequate for extrapolating beyond that range.

For example, DiDonato and Sweers observed a honeymoon period in their data that they discounted when they examined growth of heavy maintenance. Most, if not all, of the other analyses included data from all periods. If their observations apply across fleets, measured growth rates could include the effects of those early-life periods when workloads had not yet reached a mature size. While the resulting forecasting equation might adequately represent the likely workloads or costs at any time within the observation period, it might exaggerate the size of the later-life growth. The result might be that forecasts outside the sample period exaggerate the likely growth. Also possible, analyses of workloads experiencing the traditional infantile-failure pattern observed in the reliability literature might underestimate the late-life growth.

Early-life phenomena are not the only causes of variable growth rates. As an extreme example, maintenance demands cannot exceed the work required to completely disassemble an aircraft, inspect and remanufacture all its parts, then reassemble the aircraft after every use. While that extreme is highly improbable, there must be some point at which the maintenance demands can grow no further. Of course, it is also possible that workload growth will accelerate if that point is distant, as discussed in the next section. Even though researchers have not observed either phenomenon to date, such possibilities must be considered in analyses designed to extrapolate beyond current experience.

Using Linear Versus Accelerating Growth Equations

To date, each study described in this section simply assumed one of two equations for workload or cost growth: linear or compound (often called log-linear). The linear equation assumes that the workload grows like a bank account with simple interest; the annual workload increases a fixed amount each year as if the growth were a fixed percentage of the initial workload. In contrast, the compound equation assumes that the workload grows like a bank account with compound interest: The annual workload increases at a fixed percentage of the previous year's workload, including all the previous years' accumulated workload. No study tested which assumption was valid.

In the past, the difference between the two equations may have been of little consequence. So long as the results were used to estimate slow-growing workloads and costs for short periods in the future, either equation may have provided acceptably accurate estimates of the life cycle workloads or costs for a typical aircraft fleet.

Unfortunately, the difference is of great consequence when workloads must be estimated over a much longer time. As Figure 2.1 shows, the difference between typical compound- and linear-growth curves may be difficult to detect over a short time period. However, the differences may grow substantially as the aircraft fleet progresses in age. (The two curves illustrating this point were artificially constructed to double the initial workload during the first design life. If that were about 20 years, the linear rate would be 5 percent of the initial workload and the equivalent compound rate would be slightly less than 3.5 percent.) As adequate as either growth equation may be for predictions within a fleet's first design life, we need to know which equation to use for extrapolating far beyond that period.

Generalizing Across Fleets

Previous studies have taken two polar approaches to the issue of generalizing across fleets: They have assumed a single general growth rate exists that characterizes all fleets' maintenance growth, or they have assumed that each fleet's growth rate was unique. In all probability, both assumptions are partly true. On the one hand, aircraft are designed and built with similar materials that have broadly similar deterioration properties. On the other hand, some aircraft are very much more complicated and expensive, some are larger or smaller, and some are subjected to the extreme loads and

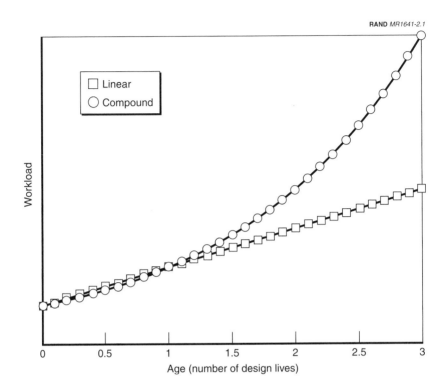

Figure 2.1 —Predictions of Linear and Compound Growth Equations for
the Second Design Life Diverge Substantially

stresses of combat. In addition to strong similarities, there may also
be strong differences.

The Air Force needs to forecast not only the workloads, availability,
and costs of individual aging fleets, but to evaluate different fleet
mixes, some of which may include fleets with little or no history to
extrapolate. With such forecasts, it can consider the wisdom of replacing an aging fleet with a younger one, perhaps gaining additional
availability while reducing annual Operations and Support costs.

Thus, it is important to know whether different fleets have different
growth rates and what fleet characteristics may affect those rates.
The different growth rates measured in previous studies for different

fleets may arise from unrelated environmental influences, or they may really reflect differences in complexity, size, material composition, or design goals.

If the growth rates have no systematic relationship to underlying fleet characteristics, it will be difficult to predict future costs for fleets that have not existed for the 10–20 years. Thus, we would also like to know whether some underlying factor, such as mission, cost, complexity, size, or weight, is present that would allow workload levels and growth to be forecast without waiting for the historical data.

Hildebrandt and Sze (1990) constructed cross-platform analyses to permit generalizations beyond the sample population. By using a measure of aircraft complexity—flyaway cost—they were able to relate platforms' initial workloads to a measurable characteristic of any fleet. Thus, their estimates may be applied to platforms outside those in the available data set, with some confidence.

Controlling for Calendar and Organizational Effects

With the exception of the Stoll and Davis (1993) and the Francis and Shaw (2000) studies of naval aircraft workloads, previous studies also did not address how non–age-related changes introduced over time might affect the measured workload growth rates. Stoll and Davis questioned the validity of some of their measured growth rates in view of their observations of underway management process changes. Likewise, Francis and Shaw cross-checked their multiyear results against a snapshot drawn from a single year (1996) to make sure that their growth measurements were not caused by some process change.

Obviously, an effect caused by an organizational change introduced during an aircraft's history could easily be confounded with a true age effect. A one-time efficiency change or modification could easily be interpreted as a lower workload-growth rate.

Less clearly, it is also possible for organizational differences to be interpreted as age effects, if different organizations operate and maintain the same model of aircraft but have aircraft of different ages. Then any organization-unique process differences might appear to be an age-related workload effect.

Budgeting for Modification Life-Cycle Patterns

Finally, conventional wisdom has it that the Air Force budgets a fixed amount of money each year to modify its aircraft to meet new operational requirements. Even if that situation has occurred in the past, it may not occur in the future. Beginning in the 1990s, new international environmental and air traffic management requirements have emerged that specify that several USAF tanker and cargo fleets be modified. In addition, new technology has become available for those fleets that will reduce flight crews and improve operational safety. In the past, to benefit from improving technologies and to meet emerging operational requirements, the Air Force would have acquired new aircraft instead. It may be entering a new era in which it must invest greater resources to acquire and install modifications to its aging equipment. If so, both the material costs for those modifications and the labor to install them may increase.

However, published research has not addressed that possibility, perhaps partly in the belief that the modification budget is essentially fixed, making the prediction problem uninteresting. Alternatively, the lack may reflect difficulties in obtaining or analyzing historical data. Whatever the reason, we look closely at modification life-cycle patterns in the next chapter. That chapter uses the observations reported in this chapter to construct a more integrated view of how workloads and material consumption may vary. That view will be the foundation for the hypotheses examined in this study.

Chapter Three

A BROADER PERSPECTIVE: LIFE CYCLE PATTERNS, NOT INEXORABLE GROWTH

Building on previous research, this chapter suggests that no single, constant growth rate can adequately represent the ebb and flow of maintenance and modification workloads over an aircraft's life cycle, and that a number of other factors may also affect workloads and material costs. It starts with the findings of Stoll and Davis and others that different aircraft experience different growth rates for the same maintenance workload, and that different workloads have different growth rates for the same aircraft. Then, it hypothesizes that at least part of those differences may be due to the complexity or size of the aircraft. After that, it suggests that the apparent late-life acceleration observed in some workloads may be due to an intrinsic design characteristic: the intended aircraft service life. It then observes that DiDonato's honeymoon period may reflect the gradual emergence of other, intrinsically less reliable components' initial failures. It then notes the unique situation for engines whose complex, state-of-the-art design and demanding operating environment make it impossible to achieve service lives comparable to aircraft. Thus, engines' maintenance-demand patterns periodically ebb and flow as the engines receive periodic overhauls. Finally, it notes that some aircraft (or engine) components have initial design or manufacturing defects that lead to an initial infantile-failure period, when demands for some parts are initially high, until those defects are corrected. Taken together, these several processes may combine to create a wide variety of different workload life-cycle patterns.

Previous research helped suggest an underlying life-cycle pattern for maintenance; however, no research existed for modification workloads. It was hypothesized that those workloads may also grow, but that growth might be punctuated by periods when large spurts of effort would be required to incorporate features that could not have been envisioned by the original designers.

Finally, this chapter suggests that both operational stresses *and* design characteristics may accelerate or retard growth. It identifies numerous factors other than age that may confound analyses of age-related effects. Thus, it provides a perspective for explaining the causes of historical variations in workloads, costs, and fleet capability over time, including factors other than age. This perspective was the basis for the analyses that comprise the remainder of this report.

More important to policymakers, the perspective goes beyond simply explaining past events. It outlines a conceptual basis for predicting how age and other factors may affect workloads, material consumption, and aircraft availability. In particular, it identifies factors whose adjustment may reduce or offset the effects of some aging processes.

As a practical matter, this study has only begun to exploit the theoretical perspective. Data limitations have made it difficult to isolate all the complex growth patterns suggested below. Future analyses will be able to examine other aspects of this perspective more thoroughly.

Most important, the perspective suggests that maintenance and modification workloads and material consumption probably grow as aircraft age, *but not without limit.* Thus, the perspective provides a counterpoint to many of the analyses discussed in Chapter Two, which implicitly assume that the historically measured workload and material consumption growth will continue unabated forever.

This chapter outlines a theoretical perspective on how age-related processes may affect maintenance and modification workloads and material consumption over time. It identifies other factors that affect workloads in ways that may confound age effects.

SUMMARY OF THIS CHAPTER

Four age-related processes—evolving technology, escalating operational requirements, material properties, and environmental stresses—directly or indirectly affect three Air Force concerns: flight safety, combat capability, and cost. While age is not a direct cause of the four processes, it is a correlate of their cumulative effects. Thus, it reflects not only the material-degradation processes of fatigue, corrosion, and the like, but also the accumulation of regulatory changes, technology evolution, and combat tactical innovations that occur after an aircraft is designed, developed, and fielded.

If it were not for the preventive and remedial benefits of maintenance, material deterioration would drive flight safety and aircraft availability downward throughout an aircraft's service life. Because different materials have different material-degradation sensitivities to different environmental and operational stressors over time, some aircraft components require repair or replacement only as the aircraft passes its nominal service life; others require maintenance much earlier and more frequently. For materials with longer service lives, maintenance inspection and repair activities increase as an aircraft ages, enabling flaws in critical (especially flight-safety) items to be detected and the items replaced before they fail. While many components' repair workloads increase to a more-or-less steady level early in an aircraft's life cycle, maintenance workload for longer-lived components accelerates as aircraft approach and exceed their original design lives, but the rate of growth will begin to diminish sometime thereafter.

In contrast, small modifications—those intended to rectify an isolated structural flight-safety problem, update operational software, improve an existing installed component's ability to perform its task, or improve reliability—may not grow over time, particularly for those aircraft whose capabilities have been eclipsed by more-modern platforms. In contrast, larger modifications intended to add new capabilities to existing platforms or to extend the platforms' operational lives may appear episodically, as the Air Force recognizes new operational challenges or technical opportunities, or as it chooses to retain an aircraft for a prolonged service life.

Many factors other than age and its correlates affect workloads and material consumption over time. Operational tempos, mission changes, flight envelopes, and exposure to various environmental hazards directly affect the demands for maintenance workloads. Less directly, changes in organizational structure, workload location, organizational incentives, maintenance skill levels, organizational scale, material availability, and maintenance processes over time also affect aircraft maintenance workloads over time.

Some of those factors also promise partial solutions to offset the cost and combat-capability effects of aging fleets. In particular, initiatives that streamline or synchronize logistics processes hold the promise of reducing nonproductive resources and their associated costs while increasing available aircraft.

AGE IS ONLY A CORRELATE OF OTHER PROCESSES

Figure 3.1 depicts how four factors, technology, operational requirements, material properties, and environmental stresses, interact over time to cause material deterioration and create technology gaps between an aircraft and the current state of the art. To meet the material-deterioration challenge, the Air Force maintenance system inspects, replaces, repairs, and protects affected materials as needed. To meet the technology-gap challenge, the Air Force modifies aircraft so that they can meet the changing operational challenges. Modifications are also made as a way of avoiding shortfalls in materials for maintenance caused by diminishing manufacturing sources (DMS) as producers abandon old technologies and adopt new ones. Both the maintenance and modification activities cause workloads that emerge in various parts of the maintenance system, which consume labor, material, and time. The labor and material consumed obviously lead to budget requirements; the maintenance time also reduces the aircraft available for operations. In addition, incomplete modifications also lead to capability deficiencies, because the unmodified aircraft cannot perform some missions.

In this theoretical perspective, age does not directly affect any of the three ultimate Air Force concerns (flight safety, costs, or availability) directly. Rather, it is simply a measure of how long the two time-related processes (material-degradation and technology-gap growth) have been at work.

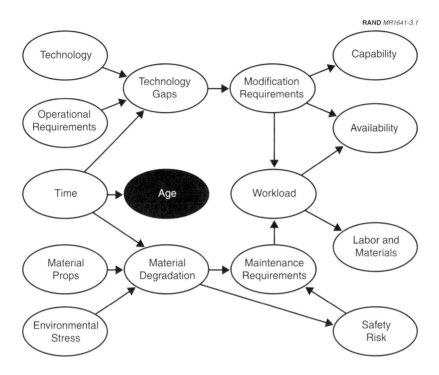

Figure 3.1—How Aircraft Aging May Relate to Flight Safety, Aircraft Availability, and Support Costs

HOW MAINTENANCE WORKLOADS MAY INCREASE AS AIRCRAFT AGE

The issue, of course, is whether and how much aircraft workloads may grow as the aircraft age, particularly if they achieve ages well beyond the Air Force's current experience. If workloads remain constant as aircraft age, labor and material costs would not increase, and availability would not decrease.

As discussed in Chapter Two, there is good evidence that maintenance workloads and material consumption increase as aircraft age. That chapter also identified five issues raised for generalizing those findings to other aircraft or to fleets whose ages extend far beyond the range of prior experience: (1) identifying constant versus variable growth patterns; (2) using linear versus accelerating growth equations; (3) generalizing across fleets; (4) controlling for calendar and organizational effects; and (5) budgeting for modification life-cycle patterns. The remainder of this section suggests how each of those five issues may affect future fleet workloads and costs.

Identifying Constant Versus Variable Growth Patterns

All aircraft are composed of a wide variety of components. The reliability and maintainability characteristics of those components vary just as widely: Some components last a long time; others do not. Some components require very expensive, bulky, and specialized maintenance equipment; others do not. Some components are easily removed from the aircraft for inspection and repair; others are not.

Aircraft components, the individual parts used to construct or outfit an aircraft, typically exhibit unique service lives that are measured in flying hours or calendar time, which means that they generally fail after an initial period of service. When they fail, maintenance personnel replace them with an identical component or repair them to extend their service lives. The replacement or repair is generally expected to give the newly installed component a service life approximately as long as that of the original component. Viewed over a long enough time in a stable operational environment, most components exhibit more or less stable mean times between failure (MTBF). (As a practical matter, changes in operational use, mission requirements or environmental stresses often cause MTBFs to vary widely over time [Crawford, 1988; Pyles and Shulman, 1995].)

Maintenance workload, the annual labor measured in manhours required to maintain an acceptable level of aircraft availability, grows as aircraft age, because scientists, engineers, and production teams have not been able to make all components' service lives identical. Unlike Oliver Wendell Holmes' poetic wonderful one-hoss shay, which lasted one hundred years to a day (Holmes, 1858), aircraft inevitably contain components with widely varying MTBFs: Tires last for only a few dozen sorties; computer circuitboards may last hundreds of flying hours; aircraft structural frames and skins are expressly designed to last many thousands of flying hours, depending on the stresses encountered in typical flight operations.

Moreover, the initial maintenance-free service lives of apparently identical components vary widely as a result of inevitable variations in material, production processes, and the operational stresses they encounter. Subtle variations in chemical makeup, heating and cooling processes, environmental exposure, or in-flight stresses all affect cumulative material deterioration.

In the particular case of aircraft, structural components are designed to achieve specific service lives, or *design service objective* (DSO), assuming a particular spectrum of in-flight stresses. Using their knowledge of the selected materials' fatigue-growth characteristics, engineers use finite-element mechanical models of stresses and empirically based models of fatigue growth to estimate how long it would take for an improbably large, but barely visible, flaw to grow to a critical point at which the metal part would fail. The initial flaw size is assumed to be large to allow for some dispersion in the size of actual flaws. Thus, individual components and aircraft may be flown safely past the DSO, but they face an increasing risk of failure past that point. Designers then adjust the design of each aircraft structural component until the expected service life exceeds the aircraft DSO. In addition, they subject individual components and a test aircraft to tests intended to simulate one or more service lives under the given set of stresses. Should items fail during those tests, they may be redesigned to achieve the service life. In that way, engineers reduce the risk that any structural component on the aircraft will fail before the DSO is reached.

The load spectra and flight envelope are specified when the design is started, so the DSO is normally expressed in flying hours. A typical fighter's DSO might be 8,000 hours; a large cargo aircraft may have an expected structural life between 20,000 and 60,000 flying hours.

Even though the DSO is specified in flying hours, many force planners refer to it in equivalent calendar time. Thus, a fighter flying 300 hours per year will reach its DSO in 25–30 years, assuming no mission-mix change or aircraft reconfiguration, making it possible to translate the DSO into an expected aircraft service life, at least with regard to structural components.

Of course, the DSO and the resulting service life depend critically on the accuracy of the estimated flight profile. The life may be shortened or extended by changes in the aircraft configuration, tactics, and mission. For example, the Air Force's decision to use B-52s for high-altitude launch of cruise missiles instead of for low-altitude penetration of enemy airspace made it possible to extend that fleet's structural life until 2040.

The service lives of other aircraft components—for example, seals, hydraulic lines, composite materials, wiring, insulators, integrated circuits, and electrical connectors—cannot be computed so directly, because so little is known about the other environmental stresses they will encounter in service or the material properties and their resilience to those stresses. Nevertheless, design engineers apply historically tested rules of thumb where possible to ensure that sufficient material is present to approach or exceed the DSO. Where that is not possible, they develop time-change policies that ensure that maintenance actions preclude potential flight-safety–related failures to the extent possible.

Of course, many aircraft components cannot be designed to last 25 to 30 years or longer. Some components, such as those in aircraft engines, use metals as do aircraft structures, but their operating environments are so harsh and the performance requirements are so high that their expected service lives are much shorter than those for aircraft structures. Components such as tires use much less durable materials than do engines and aircraft structures because a more durable substitute with the appropriate operating characteristics is simply not available.

Some failures are caused by factors other than component material selection and stresses, such as accidents, lightning strikes, foreign-object damage (FOD), or other extraordinary stresses that could not be foreseen when the aircraft was originally designed and produced.

As a consequence of this diverse range of maintenance needs, the Air Force has developed a maintenance and support infrastructure composed of equally diverse elements. Some elements are relatively modest, portable, inexpensive tools at the flightline; others are less-portable specialized equipment in base-level intermediate maintenance shops away from the flightline; still others are special fixed facilities and equipment located in centralized depots or contractor facilities far removed from flightline operations. Some maintenance occurs on the aircraft, but some work on removable components occurs in intermediate shops, the depots, or contractor facilities. Some on-aircraft work occurs at the flightline, but some requires that the aircraft be flown to a specialized depot or contractor facility. The location of the work depends on both the frequency of failure (i.e., the MTBF) and the cost and portability of the needed maintenance equipment or facilities.

Maintenance workloads arise in two forms: repairs to restore an aircraft or a component to service, and inspections to detect potential *future* failures in advance of failure. Inspections that detect future failures may result in an immediate repair being done or they may not. In some cases, the potential failure may be so remote (in time or flying hours) that maintenance personnel can safely wait until the next scheduled inspection.

The critical difference between repairs and inspections is that repairs typically occur only when components fail or are predicted to fail in the near future; inspections typically start well before expected failure and recur periodically until the part finally fails (or is predicted to fail before the next inspection). For structural components designed to meet the aircraft DSO, failures would be expected to peak at some point well past the DSO, depending on actual variations in initial flaw sizes and operating stresses. If kept until failure, the individual components' workloads would rise to a peak sometime after the DSO, then would diminish until sometime after another DSO had occurred. Because all the aircraft components share the same DSO, their repair workloads may peak at similar times. To detect those failures before they affect flight safety, inspections of DSO components usually begin well in advance of the expected failure. Therefore, inspections accumulate (across the multiple components) more rapidly as the aircraft DSO approaches.

If aircraft were kept long enough, the inspections and repair of DSO components might be expected to subside once all the repairs were accomplished. Indeed, if the aircraft were substantially refurbished to like-new condition, the aircraft workload might be expected to simply repeat the cycle. For example, the Air Force initiative to refurbish several Boeing 707 aircraft retired from commercial service for use in the Joint Strategic Targeting and Reconnaissance System

(JSTARS) fleet was hoping to reset the clock on those aircraft so that they could be used for an extended second life.

Of course, the clock cannot be reset completely to zero without disassembling the aircraft, remanufacturing all the aircraft's components, and reassembling the aircraft. Such a Herculean effort probably is not necessary for extending an aircraft's service life, because designers consider design criteria other than fatigue. Often, those other requirements virtually ensure that failures will not occur until many times the DSO; consequently, some DSO components' inspection and repair workloads will not emerge until well after the DSO.

Engines and other components also have DSOs, but they are only a fraction of the overall aircraft DSO (Athearn, Black, and Chutek, 1998; Pratt & Whitney, 1998; USAF, 1998; USAF, Oklahoma City Air Logistics Center, 1998). For example, scheduled inspections for fighter engines occur every 4,000 to 6,000 *heat cycles,* the number of times an engine's temperature passes through a critical level, as recorded by onboard engine monitors. (The operational integrity of the engine seals deteriorates with the friction generated as engine loads are increased and decreased.) As a rule of thumb, a typical fighter sortie generates 2.5 heat cycles, and most peacetime training sorties last about one hour. Therefore, fighter engines may be removed for scheduled inspection every 1,600 to 2,400 flying hours, compared with a DSO of about 8,000 flying hours for a typical fighter.

Thus, one would expect an aircraft fleet's engine repair workload to surge periodically, at a frequency depending on the fleet's flying program. Fighters nominally fly 300 hours per year, so scheduled engine removals might peak every five to eight years. Jet engines for other fleets have similar cyclic inspection programs, although at much lower rates (as low as one removal per 10,000 flying hours).

The second engine overhaul workload surge can also be expected to exceed the first, because some components, especially those most difficult to reach, disassemble, repair, and reinstall, have design service lives that far exceed two inspection cycles. Thus, some components may be designed for 20,000 cycles before any failures appear, so they will typically not require as much attention and effort in the first scheduled inspection as in later inspections. In this view, a cyclic engine maintenance workload would be anticipated to have peaks that would increase with each cycle and to have valleys that would be filled with unscheduled workloads that may or may not grow as the engines age.

The remaining components' MTBFs are typically far below the DSO. Thus, they will go through many maintenance cycles (remove, repair, and replace) before an aircraft reaches its DSO. Viewed in the aggregate, those components' maintenance workloads grow from a very low level in the initial years after an aircraft fleet is fielded to what appears to be a stable, mature level.

Figure 3.2 depicts the resulting workload pattern of these multiple processes (random failures, airframe and other DSO component inspections, DSO component repairs, short-lived non-DSO component inspection and repairs, engine inspections and repairs, and break-in maintenance). The figure reflects an assumption that the actual failure for most structural components would occur at twice the DSO. That is, each part was designed to last twice as long as the DSO, so there was little chance of a failure within the first design life.

Examining the left half of the overall curve from DSO zero to one, we can see the bathtub workload often reported by various observers. (The exaggerated engine workload makes the total a bit bumpy, but we can clearly see the initial workload decline followed by a gradual growth in later life.) After an initial period of infantile failures, the residual, or mature, workloads grow rather slowly (with some fluctuations due to the engine overhaul workload) throughout the first design service life. As the DSO approaches, the inspection workload for DSO components begins to rise, anticipating those components' potential failures. Then, DSO component replacements and repairs begin to increase, reaching a peak sometime well after the first DSO. After that time, the structural-component repair workloads would diminish, while the associated inspection workloads would stabilize or diminish slightly. Of course, workloads for the non-DSO components would grow and stabilize early in the first design life, and the engine workloads would fluctuate periodically, depending on their utilization rate and their inspection intervals.

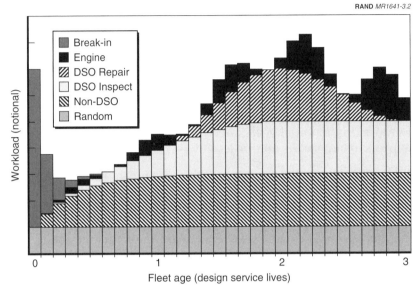

NOTE: Assumes a dispersion factor of 2 for structural fatigue and flying consistent with the original flight envelope.

Figure 3.2—Different Maintenance Workloads May Exhibit Different Patterns as Aircraft Age (not to scale)

The most speculative and controversial part of this view is the leveling off of the workload growth at some point after the first design life. As discussed in Chapter Two, analysts have not observed that hypothesized deceleration yet, because aircraft have rarely been operated much past their DSO. Thus, the empirical studies discussed in Chapter Two have typically found a generally positive growth pattern with no indication of a later deceleration of the growth rate, much less a leveling off or diminishing of the workload after some point far beyond the DSO.

At the same time, it is possible that the workload growth could accelerate before that deceleration begins. If many structural components have design characteristics that place their service lives very near the DSO, the Air Force might encounter very rapid increases in the growth of maintenance requirements as that time is approached.

Also, it is possible that new, unforeseeable, maintenance requirements will arise as aircraft are retained for longer times. For example, the Air Force may experience the effects of new material-degradation processes whose effects take longer to appear. The emergence of wiring and corrosion concerns in the aircraft engineering community over the past decade may be precursors of growing maintenance workloads.

It is also possible that the work required for each maintenance demand may increase. Most repair is composed of two activities: diagnosis and repair. Once a defect is identified, the subsequent repair action may be fairly routine. Unfortunately, aging effects may render diagnosing a problem more difficult, especially for aircraft with complex, interdependent interfaces among components. Nowhere is this situation more apparent than in avionics and flight-control systems, in which there may be multiple, difficult-to-observe, failure modes that cause similar failure symptoms. Thus, it is possible that at least some workloads may grow, even when ultimate failures remain constant. That is, the mean time to repair (MTTR) may increase, even though the MTBF is stable.

Thus, the life cycle pattern depicted in Figure 3.2 can be viewed as only one of several patterns that may emerge. Specifically, one would expect different patterns to emerge for different shops and material categories. The empirical analyses described in the rest of this report seek to identify early indicators of long-term growth. To do so, they must ensure that the long-term growth estimates are not contaminated by early-life phenomena. Those empirical analyses will expressly account for the possibility that either break-in or honeymoon phenomena may occur early in aircraft life cycles.

Material Consumption May Grow Differently Than Maintenance Workload

Conventional wisdom dictates that material consumption patterns may mimic maintenance-workload patterns as aircraft age, and that base-level material consumption would change in proportion to base maintenance workloads. For some workloads, this may be true—but not for others. For example, some aircraft-servicing activities that periodically top off fluid levels (oxygen, nitrogen, oil, etc.) may not increase in frequency or labor hours, but only in the amount of material required to top off a leaky system. Alternatively, maintenance work to diagnose and correct intermittent failures of a complex sub-system may increase dramatically as aircraft age, but it may generate only minimal material requirements (e.g., for a replacement pin, plug, or fitting). Thus, the empirical analyses address material consumption growth separately from workload growth, where possible.

Linear Versus Accelerating Growth Equations Must Be Considered

As discussed in Chapter Two, the model of how growth in workload occurs—linear or accelerating/compound—has substantial implications for future aging fleets' workloads and costs. If the underlying work grows at an accelerating rate as fleets age, those fleets' maintenance costs may become unbearable. All else being equal, the simpler model, which assumes no acceleration, is preferred not only because it is more easily computed or that it estimates a lower workload growth in late life, but because it suggests a fairly simple explanation for how workloads may grow. Specifically, if we imagine that each aircraft in a fleet is composed of components whose first maintenance requirement emerges slowly over time, and that the components' initial service lives are uniformly distributed over the aircraft's life cycle, then the workload would grow linearly as more and more components began to fail.

The pattern in Figure 3.2 contradicts these assumptions during some life-cycle periods. If that view is correct, some maintenance workloads and costs may accelerate, at least as the fleet approaches the DSO. Structural components' inspection and repair workloads (performed during programmed depot maintenance) would be expected to accelerate before they decelerate. The empirical analyses in this report seek to clarify whether workloads or material consumption accelerates (or decelerates) over an aircraft's service life.

Generalizing Across Fleets Will Enable Forecasting of Newer Fleets' Workloads

Chapter Two described evidence that different aircraft fleets experience different rates of growth for different workloads, which may reflect differences in design details or operational basing and use, some of which is undoubtedly unique to the specific model of aircraft being analyzed.

But the Air Force needs to predict those costs before they arise, especially for newer fleets. They need to know whether an underlying pattern may be present that explains a substantial portion of the growth differences across fleets—aircraft characteristics that can be known early enough in an aircraft's life cycle to indicate how fast its maintenance workloads may grow. We imagine two such broad characteristics: aircraft complexity and aircraft mission. A more complex aircraft poses greater challenges during the repair process than does a simpler one. Maintainers will find it more difficult to isolate problems on an aircraft composed of more components or on one with more interdependencies among the various components. With more ways for the failure to be remote from the symptom, the more-complex aging aircraft may experience higher workload growth than the simpler one.

As for aircraft mission, fighters obviously will experience much more rough, demanding flight envelopes than will a typical cargo aircraft. They are more likely to be flown beyond the design flight envelope, and more often. Bombers on low-level-penetration missions and helicopters on search-and-rescue or special-operations missions may also experience greater stresses relative to their design limits. Even command and control aircraft and tankers may experience differential stresses such as flying the aircraft in racetrack patterns for large portions of their operational lives, that accelerate or decelerate age-related maintenance growth.

Effects of Calendar and Organizational Transitions Can Be Mistaken for Age

Unfortunately, many factors other than aircraft age change over time and also affect workloads, costs, readiness, and flight safety. Maintenance and modification processes change when the maintenance organization, training, or incentives change, leading both to workload displacements across shops and to changes in the actual workloads (as capital investments, learning, and organizational incentives affect individuals' productivity). The pricing of labor and material has an obvious effect on the costs measured over time, and changes to prices paid by wings can change demand levels, as was demonstrated when DLR repair was changed from free issue to a fee-for-service in the early 1990s. Changes in operational requirements may increase the stresses that cause increased maintenance. Finally, changes in organization, training, and incentives can have a strong effect on the behavior of maintenance personnel at all echelons.

We need only examine some of the changes introduced over the last decade of the twentieth century to appreciate how workloads may be affected by factors other than age.

Air Force Actions Have Changed Reported Maintenance and Modification Workloads Over the 1990s. The following changes have been introduced over the past decade and may confound a historical study of age-related maintenance workload or cost growth:

- Active fighter wings were reduced to 54 Primary Aircraft Authorized (PAA) from 72 PAA, thereby reducing the unit scale and, possibly, productivity. Other wings have also been downsized, although the specific numbers vary.

- Most Active and Reserve units were reorganized into objective wings, separating on-equipment personnel into three different squadrons, further reducing maintenance scale.

- Most Active and many Reserve and Guard units began deploying partial wings in support of increased peacekeeping and other taskings, further reducing both maintenance scale and on-the-job training opportunities as more-experienced personnel are deployed.

- Compared with 1980–1989 levels, unit maintenance personnel levels have been reduced.

- Constraints placed on enlisted-personnel induction in the early 1990s, higher peacetime OPTEMPOs, and a robust domestic economy made it difficult to acquire and retain a sufficient number of skilled base-level (5-Level) journeymen technicians, leaving more work to be performed by less-experienced, less-productive (3-Level) apprentices throughout the 1990s.

- Reduced spares levels (both peacetime operating stocks and war reserve materials) during a period of retrenchment in the mid-

1990s may have induced base maintenance personnel to attempt repairs that could have been performed more efficiently at depots. That may have also increased maintenance workloads as maintenance personnel cannibalized needed parts from other aircraft or major assemblies.

- The change from free-issue stocks for DLRs to direct unit-level funding (called DLR funding) was intended in part to encourage increased component-repair efforts at the base level.

- The change from direct funding of aircraft PDM in AFMC's budget to incorporating the funding in MAJCOMs' budgets reportedly caused a workload shift from depot PDM shops to unit-level phased- and isochronal-inspection shops.

- DLR funding also caused depot shops to improve their tracking of actual costs, both labor and material. That more-disciplined recording of material consumption may have increased DLR repair prices.

- An AFMC policy change to discontinue job-routing of subassemblies (called shop reparable units, or SRUs) may have caused apparent increases in the cost of repairing larger units, ranging from line replaceable units (LRUs) to whole engines.

- An Air Force policy to move some base-level avionics and engine repair to the depots may have caused increases in the depot workloads and may have offset age-related increases in base-level intermediate shop workloads.

- The Air Force separated modification budgets from depot-level maintenance in 1989. To the extent that modifications are less closely synchronized with PDMs, this action may have increased modification workloads. (Previously, modifications exploited the fact that PDMs disassembled major portions of the aircraft to minimize the modification workload. The depots have continued to synchronize both workloads where possible, but the funding and timing of different work may not be so closely synchronized.)

- In the last half of the 1990s, the Air Force closed two depots, San Antonio Air Logistics Center (SA-ALC) and Sacramento ALC (SM-ALC), moving and consolidating work across the three remaining ALCs. This action may have led to decreased productivity at the receiving depots, as shops were rearranged to accommodate new workloads, technicians were trained to perform unfamiliar work on unfamiliar aircraft and parts, and unanticipated capacity and material-requirements problems emerged.

- Additional maintenance and modification workloads were allocated to new contractors, who had shop start-up, training, and capacity problems similar to the ALCs'.

- Interim contractor support (ICS) has been extended for two of the newest aircraft mission designs, the B-1 and the C-17.

These initiatives and actions were undertaken to address particular challenges the Air Force faced at the time. Their ultimate outcomes may work to the long-term benefit of the service. However, they serve to confound any analysis that relies solely on time-sequenced historical data to estimate the effects of age on maintenance and modification workloads and material consumption.

MODIFICATION LIFE-CYCLE PATTERNS MAY DIFFER FROM MAINTENANCE PATTERNS

Modifications also affect maintenance workloads. They differ only in that they reconfigure the aircraft instead or restoring it to its prior configuration. Field, depot, or contractor maintenance personnel using their normal maintenance facilities typically install most modifications. Manufacturers of the modification kits often use the same personnel and facilities they would use for making new or replacement components.

Why then, should we care to distinguish between the two activities? The distinction is important in this study because the age-related patterns of modification demands may differ from the patterns discussed above for maintenance. In particular, flight-safety and service-life-extension modifications may increase sharply as the original aircraft DSO is approached. In addition, some fleets will occasionally need major system modifications to meet unforeseen operational demands as new technologies or the capabilities of new opponents emerge.

Designers' Horizons Limit the Operational Usefulness and Supportability of Their Original Designs

Aging aircraft may experience increasing modification workloads because the designers have only imperfect knowledge about future requirements when the aircraft is first designed—specifically,

* how an aircraft will be used in actual operations

* what new aircraft capabilities may be required in future operations

* what future technological changes may occur.

Thus, the operational demands and technology baseline originally envisioned by the designer may change as an aircraft fleet ages, as depicted by the dashed line in Figure 3.3. As operational personnel develop tactics to exploit a new aircraft's capabilities, it is not uncommon for them to exceed the flight envelope used to evaluate the original design. As enemies develop countermeasures for a new aircraft's original capabilities, it is not uncommon for operators to request modifications to surmount those challenges. As the commercial-air marketplace evolves, its requirements, not uncommonly, affect operational requirements for military aircraft. As the industrial base evolves, it is common to replace an older technology with a newer one, rendering the replaced technology less available, more expensive, or even non-existent.

Thus, the aircraft's original capabilities may actually exceed the operational requirements when it is first fielded, but those requirements will almost certainly expand. Over time, the fleet's system program managers and system designers will take periodic actions to close the resulting gap. Thus, Figure 3.3 shows a steadily growing requirement line. The aircraft's capabilities exceed that line initially. A series of subsequent modifications helps the aircraft catch up with or stay ahead of requirements.

Aircraft modifications take one of three forms: (generally major) system modifications that change the basic aircraft design and ca-

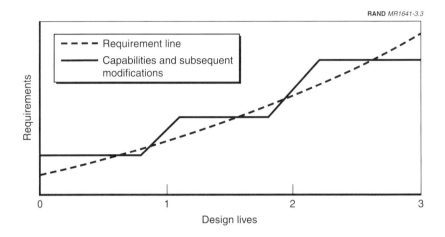

Figure 3.3—Evolving System Requirements Trigger Episodic Modification Actions as Aircraft Age

pabilities, (generally minor) component improvements, and software modifications that change computer programs or technical procedures. System modifications often involve changes to an aircraft's physical structure (e.g., frame, carriage, surface areas) or to its infrastructure (e.g., wiring, hydraulic systems); component modifications usually change only one or a few easily removed elements with replacements that have the same form, fit, and function. Software changes generally require no material changes at all; they extend the aircraft's capabilities by incorporating improved parameters (e.g., to reflect recently measured bomb trajectories or radar characteristics), new algorithms that exploit available equipment more thoroughly, or new operating or maintenance procedures that modify the aircraft's stresses or exposure to those stresses. Obviously, some modifications may occur in tandem, as when a software change is made to exploit the capabilities of newly modified components.

Changing Operational Requirements May Cause Episodic System Modification Workloads

The requirements for all three kinds of modifications emerge gradually over time. Smaller, less-expensive changes, such as component and software modifications, might be incorporated equally gradually, although they may increase and accelerate with age. Because that work is inherently less expensive and less disruptive to training and operations than are major aircraft modifications, it might be budgeted and scheduled as a fairly steady workload.

In contrast, major system modifications generally require removing an aircraft from service to extensively alter the aircraft structure or infrastructure (wiring, plumbing, etc.). They are also typically several times more expensive than component modifications, if only because they replace many aircraft components at once and require substantial disassembly of portions of the aircraft for the work to be performed. This disassembly leads, in turn, to a situation whereby several major system changes may be incorporated nearly simultaneously to position the aircraft for continued use for a foreseeably long period. We can imagine, therefore, a series of fairly large episodic expenditures as major modifications are incorporated over the aircraft life cycle.

The size and scope of each subsequent major system change may be larger than those of its predecessor. Whereas early modifications will respond to fairly small discrepancies between requirements and capabilities by modifying a few related components, later modifications may need to address larger discrepancies. In addition, later changes may find that the cumulative effects of prior changes make it necessary to introduce a much more widespread modification, which may require changes to many more aircraft subsystems. Thus, the periodic series of system-modification workload surges in Figure 3.4 increases in size, and the workload for software and component modifications that fluctuate less violently than the system modifications grows steadily.

As a practical matter, it seems unlikely that the major modifications would occur exactly at the DSO. Rather, we can imagine that they will occur whenever a new requirement emerges from the operational environment. To the extent that designers and engineers can foresee those requirements, they will try to forestall the need for future modifications by incorporating as many as possible in each major modification, further heightening the size of each modification-workload surge.

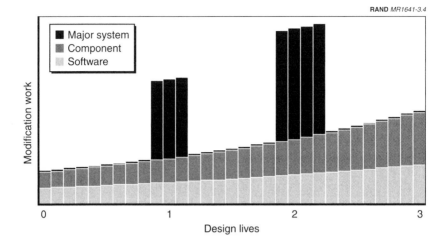

**Figure 3.4—Aircraft Modifications May Fluctuate Widely as Fleets Age
(not to scale)**

Chapter Four

ESTIMATING AGE-RELATED WORKLOAD AND MATERIAL GROWTH: APPROACH

This study tested many, but not all, the theoretical concepts of life cycle maintenance and modification workload patterns suggested in Chapter Three against historical USAF aircraft data. In addition, it measured those patterns so that future workloads and material consumption levels could be forecast for both existing and future fleets. In particular, this study examined historical USAF maintenance and modification data for the presence and size of

1. late-life workload (or material-consumption) growth

2. late-life workload acceleration or deceleration

3. early-life honeymoons or infantile failures

4. differences across workload or material-consumption categories

5. relationships between aircraft size or complexity (as measured by flyaway cost) and late-life workload growth

6. exogenous, calendar-related, events and trends

7. cyclic surges in major modification workloads.

Data limitations precluded examining USAF experience regarding

1. cyclic engine workloads

2. modification material requirements

3. software modifications.

SUMMARY OF THIS CHAPTER

The analyses discussed in this report applied ordinary least squares multiple regression techniques to 13 different workload and material-consumption categories. Each workload or material-consumption category was analyzed separately to exploit the available data as much as possible.

The 13 categories include work performed by base-level maintenance personnel (flightline maintenance, intermediate maintenance, periodic inspections, and special inspections), depot-level maintenance personnel (DLR repair, PDM, engine overhaul, Time Change Technical Orders), and contractor logistics support (CLS). They also included base-level consumption of consumable (known as General Stock Division, or GSD) material, replacement of support equipment, and modernization of DLRs.

Four other workload and material categories were identified for which no historical data were found: over-and-above depot maintenance, unscheduled depot-level maintenance, modification material design and fabrication, and software maintenance. Those categories' life cycle patterns were not examined.

Data sources were identified for each of the 13 categories. For base-level personnel workloads, the data source presented a detailed reporting of annual workloads for several years by aircraft MDS and MAJCOM. Other workload and material-consumption data sources never recorded data by MAJCOM. In a few cases (DLR repair, GSD, equipment replacement), data were reported by MDS, but some cross-MDS aggregation had been allocated on a "fair share" basis to develop those values. DLR modernization investments were available at only the MD level.

Regression equations were developed for each workload and material-consumption category. All equations included age, flyaway cost, the age–flyaway cost interaction term (i.e., the product of the two) and four break-in–period terms as independent variables. Other variables, including a calendar (year) variable, MAJCOM, basic mission, PDM interval, cross-fleet age differences, were included in the initial regression, if those data were available.

After examining the full regression, we used a stepwise backward regression approach to eliminate statistically nonsignificant terms. We then added a second-order variable centered on age 20 to the result to detect and measure any late-life acceleration or deceleration.

The final regression results were tested for the presence of data points that might have an undue influence on the regression coefficients. Where such points were detected, they were removed and the entire procedure was repeated, beginning with the initial full regression. When the revised regressions yielded different regression results, the potential causes of the extraordinary data points were examined.

WORKLOAD AND MATERIAL-CONSUMPTION CATEGORIES

The analysis considered only aircraft maintenance and modification workloads and material use. Nonmaintenance workloads, such as medical support and supply management, were excluded, as were maintenance of facilities and equipment other than aircraft. We identified 17 workload or material-consumption categories and organized them according to work content—i.e., maintenance or modification; performing organization—i.e., base, contractor, or depot; and location—on-equipment or off-equipment. Material-consumption costs associated with each workload category were analyzed separately from the workloads themselves.

Maintenance Workloads and Material Consumption Were Categorized According to Work Content and Maintenance Echelon

In view of previous research, discussed in Chapter Two, and the different life-cycle patterns suggested in Chapter Three, the analysis sought to measure how growth might vary across different workload or material-consumption categories. It also distinguished modification workloads from maintenance workloads at both base and depot. Finally, bases' material consumption was separated from maintenance and modification workloads. Although we may anticipate that both aspects might grow as aircraft age, there is no reason to expect that the two patterns will be identical. (Unfortunately, no material-consumption data for depot workloads were available when this research was conducted.)

The Categories Reflect Three Activities: Modernization, Operations and Maintenance, and Military Personnel Training

As shown in Table 4.1, the categories reflect traditional activity and cost categories such as those in the Air Force budget. However, the table is organized to emphasize how each category is related to one of two different Air Force activities: modernizing the existing fleet or operating and maintaining that fleet. In addition, the table distinguishes between the maintenance activities performed by nonmilitary organizations and those performed specifically by military personnel. Thus, it shows not only the traditional distinction between base and depot maintenance, but also work performed under contractor logistics support (CLS) contracts.

In the last column, the table identifies how each of these activities is related to cost elements identified in the OSD Cost Analysis Improvement Group (CAIG) cost framework (OSD, 1992). The framework in this study is slightly more detailed than the CAIG framework for base maintenance personnel and DLR budgets because different workload growth patterns were expected for different repair workloads subsumed in single categories in the CAIG framework (e.g., component repair intermediate maintenance versus on-equipment periodic inspections). If this study expectation is correct, some maintenance-workload categories may grow more quickly than others in the same CAIG category, thus causing analysts and forecasters to underestimate the overall growth pattern when extrapolating beyond the period for which historical data are available.

The first four categories (flightline, intermediate, phased or isochronal inspections, and special inspections) reflect four different kinds of operations and maintenance support work performed by manned aerospace maintenance enlisted and civilian personnel (Air Force Specialty Code 2A). Flightline workloads reflect work per-

Table 4.1

Labor and Material Categories for Maintenance and Modification

Purpose	Workload or Material-Consumption Category	Corresponding AFCAIG Cost-Analysis Category
Operations & Maintenance (Military Personnel)	Flightline Maintenance	1.2, base maintenance
	Intermediate Maintenance	1.2, 3.1, base maintenance, intermediate centralized maintenance
	Base Periodic Inspections	1.2, 3.1
	Special Inspections	1.2, 3.1
Operations & Maintenance (Nonmilitary Personnel & Material)	DLR Repair	2.3,[a] DLR consumption
	General Stock Division (GSD)	2.2, 3.2, GSD consumption
	Equipment Replacement	
	Programmed Depot Maintenance	4.1, PDM
	Over-and-Above Depot Maintenance	4.1, PDM
	Unscheduled Depot-Level Maintenance	4.1, PDM
	Depot Engine Overhaul	
	Contractor Logistics Support (CLS) per Aircraft	5.2, CLS
	Contractor Logistics Support (CLS) per Flying Hour	5.2, CLS
Modernization	Modification Design and Fabricate	6.2, Modification
	Time Change Technical Orders (TCTOs)	6.2, Modification
	Software Maintenance	6.5,[b] Software Maintenance
	DLR & SSD Replacement & Modernization	2.3,[a] DLR Consumption

[a]Commands' DLR consumption is budgeted as a single operations and maintenance cost. It was divided here into two parts, one for repair of currently owned DLRs and another for the modernization of DLRs. Neither of these categories includes the overhead for managing, storing, retrieving, and distributing DLRs.

[b]Software Maintenance is normally budgeted as part of sustaining support from the contractor or third-party suppliers. It is categorized as part of the modification activity, because it is primarily an activity to incorporate new features and capabilities in an existing aircraft.

formed between sorties on the aircraft at the flightline, including fairly non-invasive inspections of the aircraft and its major systems, low-level unscheduled maintenance (topping up fluids, repairing cosmetic damage, etc.), and repairing failures of mission-critical subsystems by removing and replacing line replaceable units (LRUs) and consumable components.

In the USAF logistics community, the term *intermediate mainte-nance* traditionally includes a wide range of different maintenance activities that are performed away from the flightline. The activities are dominated in sheer labor consumption by the component repair shops' diagnosis and repair of LRUs and whole engines that were removed from aircraft during flightline maintenance. However, such maintenance also includes periodic detailed inspections of aircraft structures and systems based on either accumulated flying hours (phased inspections) or elapsed time (isochronal inspections). In addition, it includes headquarters-directed special inspections of aircraft in response to potential safety problems or the need to install a minor modification. Finally, it includes a number of other maintenance activities, including maintenance and management of aerospace ground equipment and transient aircraft passing through from other bases. These two final categories of maintenance were not included in this study.

Intermediate maintenance activities were separated into three cate-gories for this study, because each category's workload growth pat-terns were expected to differ. Component (including engine) repair shops were expected to experience the early initial growth associated with the non-DSO components, as described in Figure 3.2, but show only limited long-term growth. Periodic inspections, which may be scheduled on the basis of elapsed time (isochronal) or flying hours (phased) since the previous inspection, were expected to experience the greater long-term growth associated with DSO component in-spections and repair in the same figure. Finally, special inspections were expected to occur randomly throughout an aircraft's life cycle, and thus exhibit little, if any, growth. In all cases, the actual long-term growth was expected to be sensitive to the aircraft complexity, or flyaway cost.

However, intermediate-maintenance workloads were expected to exhibit the same honeymoon, break-in, and late-life deceleration ef-fects as the flightline workloads. Moreover, they were expected to exhibit similar effects of organizational and skill-level changes during the late 1990s.

In an effort to develop a comprehensive cost-management account-ing system, the Air Force Cost Analysis Improvement Group (AFCAIG) has developed a comprehensive accounting system for collecting and analyzing budgetary expenditures throughout the Air Force. One particular subset of that accounting system focuses on those expenditures associated with operating individual aircraft. The Air Force Total Operating Cost (AFTOC) accounting system uses the AFCAIG framework to collect data about the cost of operating air-craft. Those data are used to estimate marginal cost factors for wing, MAJCOM, and force-wide forecasts of operating costs under alterna-tive force structure and activity (flying hour) scenarios. The right-most column of Table 4.1 shows the AFCAIG categories correspond-ing to the workload and material-consumption categories used in this study. As shown there, all three categories of intermediate main-tenance may appear in two different AFCAIG categories, either unit maintenance (AFCAIG category 1.2) or intermediate maintenance ex-ternal to the unit (AFCAIG Category 3.1). Since only productive work is recorded, these activities do not include the specialty training ac-tivities normally recorded in personnel support (AFTOC category 7.1). The actual location (internal or external to the unit) is of no relevance to this study, because the work performed is identical in nature regardless of location.

The next eight categories (DLR repair, GSD, equipment replacement, programmed depot maintenance, over-and-above depot mainte-nance, unscheduled depot-level maintenance, depot engine over-haul, and two categories of contractor logistics support) represent operational units' demands for material and nonmilitary labor.

DLR repair represents both the labor and material needed to repair aircraft components at organic and contractor depot facilities, but it includes neither the costs of purchasing replacement or upgraded DLRs nor the cost of operating the supply management activity group (SMAG), which manages the acquisition, storage, and distri-bution of DLRs. In addition, it includes both the labor and the mate-rial components of cost, a measure we used instead of the repair la-bor hours because the labor-hours data coverage varied during the historical data period, as discussed below.

GSD procurement and equipment replacement categories include material acquisition costs for material consumed (or replacement equipment acquired) directly by the flying units, as well as costs for some common consumable materials used for modifications (e.g., seals and minor hardware) at base level. It excludes material and equipment used to support repair in the depots and at maintenance contractors.

Programmed depot maintenance is scheduled and planned inspection and repair work performed on-aircraft exclusively at the depots or their contractors. This is the workload that should most strongly exhibit the DSO component-inspection and repair-growth patterns hypothesized in Figure 3.2.

PDM budgets are planned three years in advance, using reported workload data, which are up to three years old. Often, but not always, the historical data are averaged over the previous three years to minimize transient fluctuations. As a result, the budget reflects the reported hours experienced on typical PDMs five years before the budget year. If age-related growth is present, the forecast labor hours may lag behind the actual requirement.

PDMs are composed of two different activities: a basic package of planned inspections and repairs and an "over-and-above" category of unplanned work. Over-and-above workload varies with the condition of the individual aircraft, but it consists of work whose scope is outside the basic PDM package. Only limited over-and-above data were available, so that workload was not addressed in this analysis.

In contrast, unscheduled depot-level maintenance (UDLM) represents depot aircraft workload demands that may arise unpredictably, whether from foreign object damage (FOD), operational mishaps, or environmental stresses. The workload should exhibit an almost static level, regardless of aircraft age. Again, no historical data were discovered about UDLMs, so they were not addressed in this study.

Depot engine overhauls are similar to PDMs, but they are inspections and repairs of whole engines. The overhauls of some aircraft engines occur at base level, but that workload is included in the base component repair maintenance category performed by military personnel. Because many engine components have much shorter life limits than the aircraft, the study framework suggests that the workload would have the cyclic nature shown in Figure 3.2. Unfortunately, sufficient historical data were not available to confirm that hypothesis, as we discuss below.

The Air Force often finds it cost-effective to purchase contractor logistics support for some of its aircraft, particularly those aircraft with civilian equivalents. As a practical matter, individual contracts use either or both of two different contracting compensation schemes, one based on flying hours (per-flying-hour cost) and another fixed (per-aircraft cost). When the annual maintenance requirements can be predicted reasonably accurately, regardless of flying hours, the per-aircraft contract clause covers maintenance activities. Those activities may include heavy-maintenance activities similar to isochronal inspections and PDMs, and so their late-life workloads (and costs) might grow generally like those for the DSO components in Figure 3.2.

The per-flying-hour contract clauses have maintenance requirements that vary according to the flying performed, so their annual totals depend on the planned and actual flying hours needed for the fleet. Covered maintenance activities may include OPTEMPO-related component repair, phased inspections, and even flightline maintenance in some cases. Thus, their workloads may grow similarly to non-DSO components, exhibiting workload growth only during the early portion of the life cycle.

The last four categories—modification design and fabrication, TCTOs, software maintenance, and component modernization—reflect activities the Air Force undertakes to modernize its existing fleets short of replacing them. The broader modification budget was divided into two categories so that labor to install modifications (recorded as Time-Change Technical Orders, or TCTOs) could be distinguished from the design and fabrication cost required to develop, test, and procure the needed modification kits. Long-term histories for modification kits were not available when this study was performed.

The DLR replacement and modernization budget reflects three unrelated processes:

1. The simple replacement of worn-out spare parts

2. The procurement of additional spares, where required asset levels were underestimated due to changes in demand patterns

3. The procurement of significantly redesigned spare parts (those requiring a change in the national stock number).

The first activity is dominated by the other two. Adams et al. (1993) found that factors 2 and 3, which they called *churn*, required most of the annual DLR procurement funds. In this framework, one way to modify an older system is by incremental changes to DLRs. If so, DLR replacement and modernization costs might grow as new requirements emerge that can be satisfied without a major aircraft modification.

Software maintenance is more accurately characterized as software modernization, because it requires that existing onboard computer programs be modified, by adding something as major as a new functional capability or removing something as minor as an old bug, to change the programs' operational characteristics. Just as with DLR modification, software modification is an inexpensive way to upgrade an aircraft's functional capabilities. Thus, software-modification growth may be expected to be moderate, incremental, and much smoother than major modifications.

Some of these categories' life-cycle patterns could not be examined because of limits on available data.

DATA AVAILABILITY VARIED BY WORKLOAD OR MATERIAL CATEGORY

The Air Force has no comprehensive system for historical maintenance and material consumption data. Some historical data exist only as hardcopy records kept in office file cabinets or in old reports archived sporadically. When computerized data do exist, often only the current year's data are kept, sometimes with one or two years' history or forecasts.

We were unable to find adequate historical data for two of the modernization categories—modifications design and fabrication, and software maintenance—and two of the external O&M categories—

unscheduled depot-level maintenance and over-and-above work-loads, in Table 4.1.

Data Availability Varied by Category

Data were obtained for the 13 remaining categories, but they were from different sources, covered different time periods, and used different units of measure, as shown in Table 4.2. In addition, the different sources did not cover all USAF MDS, as shown in Table 4.3.

Depending on the source, the underlying historical data also reflected varying degrees of preprocessing, which may have attenuated some age-related effects. For example, the AF Reliability and Maintainability Information System (REMIS) was least subject to that error, because the underlying data are detailed reports of actual maintenance events and tasks performed on individual aircraft (i.e., traceable to aircraft or component serial number) on a particular date at a particular location. In contrast, PDM, DLR, repair, GSD, equipment replacement, engine overhaul, Contractor Logistics Support (both aircraft- and flying-hour–based) DLR replacement and modernization, and Time-Change Technical Orders data are planned workloads or costs for "typical" aircraft. DLR repair, GSD, and equipment replacement, and engine overhaul data have the additional complication that the data are developed by aggregating demands (by stock number for DLR repair; by location for GSD and equipment replacement) across different aircraft, then allocating those demands to aircraft MDS based on flying hours, thereby blurring the demands across older and younger aircraft. Finally, the DLR replacement and modernization data were available in only the most-aggregated form, by mission design (MD).

Analysis Approach Varied by Category

Each category's historical data covered different times and fleets. Therefore, it was necessary to analyze each category separately. As discussed in detail below, some commands' or aircraft fleets' data

Table 4.2
Data Sources for Maintenance and Modification Workload

Framework Category	Source	Coverage	Units
Flightline Maintenance	AFMC, REMIS PMO, 1999	1994–1998	MMH/FH
Intermediate Maintenance	AFMC, REMIS PMO, 1999	1994–1998	MMH/FH
Phased/ Isochronal Inspections	AFMC, REMIS PMO, 1999	1994–1998	MMH/FH
Special Inspections	AFMC, REMIS PMO, 1999	1994–1998	MMH/FH
DLR Repair	RDB (D041)	1993–1999	$/FH
General Stock Division (GSD)	USAF, AFCAIG, 1998b	1999, 2001	$/FH
Equipment Replacement	USAF, AFCAIG, 1998b	1999, 2001	$/FH
Programmed Depot Maintenance	AFMC MRRB Spreadsheet, 1999	1999	DPSH/PDM
	C-130 System Program Director (SPD)	1990–1997	DPSH/PDM
	C-135 SPD, 1999	1970–1999	DPSH/PDM
	C-141 SPD	1990–1998	DPSH/PDM
	F-15 SPD	1990–1998	DPSH/PDM
	Marks & Hess (1981)	1979	DPSH/PDM
	Paulson & Hoffmayer (1980)	1977	DPSH/PDM
Over-and-Above Depot Maintenance	n.a.		
Unscheduled Depot -Level Maintenance	n.a.		
Depot Engine Overhaul	USAF, SA-ALC, 1999a	1999	dem/FH

Table 4.2—continued

Framework Category	Source	Coverage	Units
	USAF, SA-ALC, Engine PMO, 1999b	1999, 2000	DPSH/dem
Contractor Logistics Support (CLS) per aircraft	USAF, AFCAIG, 1998a	1999, 2001	$/PAA
Contractor Logistics Support (CLS) per flying hour	USAF, AFCAIG, 1998a	1999, 2001	$/FH
Modification Design and Fabricate	n.a.		
Software Maintenance	n.a.		
DLR & SSD Replacement & Modernization	USAF, 1994– 1999	1993–1999	$M/TAI
Time-Change Technical Orders (TCTOs)	REMIS GCSAS	1958–1998	DPSH/TCTO

NOTES:
MMH/FH = maintenance manhours (work accomplished) per flying hour
$/FH = average cost per flying hour
DPSH/PDM = depot product standard hours (work planned) per PDM
MRRB = Material Requirements Review Board (approves planned PDM work)
n.a. = not available
dem/FH = engine demands per flying hour (Total)
DPSH/dem = depot product standard hours (planned work) per engine demand
$/PAA = Forecast annual average cost per Primary Authorized Aircraft (per PAA)
$M/TAI = budgeted average annual cost (in million$) per total aircraft inventory (TAI)
DPSH/TCTO = planned depot product standard hours for a Time-Change Technical Order.

Table 4.3

Aircraft Included in Analyses and Category for Which Data Were Available

MDS	Fltline	Int'md	Phase	Spec	DLR(R)	GSD	PDM	DEOH	CLS(A)	CLS(F)	TCTO	DLR(P)
A-10	X	X	X	X	X	X						X
OA-10	X	X	X	X	X	X						X
B-1B	X	X	X	X	X	X	X				X	X
B-2A	X	X	X	X	X	X					X	X
B-52H		X			X	X	X	X	X		X	X
C-5A	X	X			X	X	X	X			X	X
C-5B	X	X			X	X	X	X			X	X
C-5C		X						X				X
C-9A/C						X			X			
KC-10A	X								X	X	X	
C-12C/F									X	X		
C-17A					X	X					X	X
TC-18A								X	X			
C-20A/B									X			
C-21A									X	X		
C-22B									X			
C-26B									X			
C-27A									X			
C-32A									X			
C-37A									X			
C-38A									X			
C-40B									X			
C-130E	X	X	X	X	X	X	X	X			X	X
C-130H	X	X	X	X	X	X		X				X
C-130J				X				X				
EC-130E						X		X				
EC-130H						X		X	X			X
EC-130J						X		X				
A/H/K/L/M/T/WC-130						X	X	X	X		X	X
KC-135D/E	X	X	X	X	X	X	X	X			X	X
KC-135R/T	X	X	X	X	X	X	X	X			X	X
E/O/R/WC-135	X	X	X	X		X	X	X			X	X
C-137B						X						
C-137C						X			X	X		
C-141B	X	X			X	X	X	X			X	X
E-3B	X	X	X	X	X	X		X			X	X
E-3C	X	X	X	X	X	X		X			X	X
E-4B	X	X	X	X	X	X			X			
E-8A	X											
E-8C	X	X	X	X		X		X				
E-9A									X	X		
F-4G	X	X										
F-15A	X	X	X	X	X	X	X	X			X	X
F-15C	X	X	X	X	X	X	X	X				X
F-15E	X	X	X	X	X	X	X	X			X	X
F-16A	X	X	X	X	X	X		X				X
F-16C	X	X	X	X	X	X		X			X	X
EF-111A	X	X	X	X				X			X	
F-117A	X								X			X
UH-1	X	X	X	X		X					X	X
MH-53	X	X	X	X	X	X					X	X
HH-60	X	X	X	X	X	X						X
T-1A									X	X		X
T-3A									X	X		X
T-6A									X	X		X
T-37B	X	X	X	X	X	X					X	X
T-38B	X	X	X	X	X	X					X	X
AT-38B	X	X	X	X	X	X					X	X
T-39A						X					X	X
CT-43A					X	X			X	X		X
U-2R/S	X	X	X	X								

were known to be wrong for some workloads. So they were removed from the analysis. Also discussed below, TCTO data were used to adjust the available PDM data to avoid confounding maintenance and modification workloads.

The remainder of this section presents equations used in the various regression analyses. The variables in the equations have coefficients whose values will be estimated in the next chapter. In that chapter, those coefficients are presented in tables with longer names to identify the related variable than practical in these already-complicated equations. As each variable is defined in this chapter, its name in the next chapter will be noted in parentheses. For example, the average fleet age variable, A, will be defined as

A = average aircraft fleet age, in years (FAge)

where A is the variable used in the equations and FAge is the identical variable used in the Chapter Five tables.

On-Equipment (Flightline) Data, Edits, and Regressions

The data for on-equipment flightline workloads were obtained from the Reliability and Maintainability Information System (REMIS) Performance Production Subsystem (REMIS PPS). We used a standard REMIS PPS report to retrieve annual on-equipment work performed on each major aircraft system, by MAJCOM, MDS, and block, using the standard USAF Work Unit Code (WUC) structure for each aircraft. We removed aircraft support general (i.e., phased inspections, special inspections, and shop support general) activities. Data for C-5 aircraft in 1994 were clearly underreported, because values were less than one-fourth the later years' values, so those data also were removed. Scheduled maintenance, unscheduled maintenance, and repair workloads were summed across subsystems and normalized by flying hours, for each MDS, block, command, and year.

Some readers may be concerned that these data (and the off-equipment data discussed below) are widely reported to exhibit under-recording biases. This analysis assumes that those errors do not vary over time or across aircraft *within* a major command. As discussed below, specific statistical controls have been introduced to detect systematic differences *across* commands, missions, or time. If anything, systematic force-wide underreporting would cause this analysis to underestimate the size of any workload growth.

REMIS reports not only the maintenance performed at operational units but also maintenance performed in the Air Force Material Command and at some allies' overseas bases (mostly for F-16 aircraft). Those relatively sparse observations were excluded from the analysis as atypical of normal USAF operations.

Average fleet ages were derived for each MDS, block, and major command fleet from data extracted from the Air Force Program Data System as of December 31, 1999. Ages were then computed for each analysis record by adjusting the 1999 average age by the difference between 1999 and the data year.

The on-equipment regression analysis included several control variables to ensure that factors other than age did not exaggerate or diminish the relationship between age and on-equipment workload. The first of these were variables to detect and measure early-life effects unique to the initial period when the Air Force is breaking in the fleet. The exact shapes and durations of those early-life periods is unknown, so four early-life "break-in" variables were constructed to detect and measure DiDonato and Sweer's (1997) honeymoon effect or any infantile failures. Two were simple pulse variables, one covering the first five years and the other covering the first ten years. The other two were diminishing-ramp factors covering the same periods. Figure 4.1 displays all four break-in variables graphically. The two pulse break-in variables, B1 and B2, take on the value 1.0 when the fleet age is less than five years and ten years, respectively. Expressed in equation form, they are

$$B_1 = \begin{cases} 1 & 0 \le A \le 5 \\ 0 & \text{elsewhere} \end{cases} \tag{4.1}$$

and

$$B_2 = \begin{cases} 1 & 0 \le A \le 10 \\ 0 & \text{elsewhere} \end{cases} \tag{4.2}$$

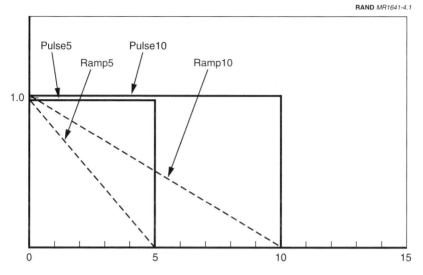

RAND *MR1641-4.1*

Figure 4.1—Most Regressions Used Both Pulse and Diminishing-Ramp Variables to Detect and Measure Break-In Effects

where

A = average aircraft fleet age, in years (FAge)

B_1 = 5-year pulse variable (Pulse5)

B_2 = 10-year pulse variable (Pulse10).

The two diminishing-ramp variables, B_3 and B_4 initially have the value 1.0 at age zero, but they decrease linearly to zero by age five or ten, respectively. Expressed in equation form, they are

$$B_3 = \begin{cases} \dfrac{5-A}{5} & 0 \le A \le 10 \\ 0 & \text{otherwise} \end{cases} \qquad (4.3)$$

and

$$B_4 = \begin{cases} \dfrac{10-A}{10} & 0 \le A \le 10 \\ 0 & \text{otherwise} \end{cases} \qquad (4.4)$$

where

B_3 = 5-year diminishing-ramp variable (Ramp5)

B_4 = 10-year diminishing-ramp variable (Ramp10).

In addition to the break-in variables, categorical (0/1) variables were constructed for fleets' basic mission and operating command. Complete life histories were not available for each MDS or block. As a consequence, early experiments using categorical variables for each MDS and block not only detected and measured workload variations caused by MDS-unique characteristics such as like design variations, they also attributed effects due to age differences to the MDS or block. Instead of using categorical variables for each MDS in this analysis, we constructed categorical variables only at the major mission area, including bomber, cargo, tanker, fighter, helicopter, trainers, command and control, and reconnaissance mission areas. These categorical variables were constructed to measure how workloads differed from fighters. Thus, the size of their coefficients would measure how much more (or less) workload each basic mission aircraft fleet experienced per flying hour than fighters, on average. At that level of detail, most missions had at least some older and some younger aircraft fleets. (This choice also enhances the generalizability of the results to fleets beyond those in the available data.)

Categorical variables were also constructed for each major operating command other than the Air Combat Command (ACC). Any difference in operating concept or reporting procedures in Air Education and Training Command (AETC), Air Forces in Europe (AFE), Pacific Air Forces (PACAF), Air Mobility Command (AMC), Air National Guard (ANG), or Air Force Reserves (AFR) would not be misconstrued as age-related workload growth. Thus, each command other than ACC would have a categorical variable, and a coefficient for that variable would represent how that command's workload differs from that of ACC, on average.

As a further way to distinguish the effects of aircraft design from age, the aircraft flyaway cost was also used as an explanatory variable. To determine whether workloads for larger, more complex, more expensive aircraft grow more rapidly than others, an age-cost interaction variable was also constructed.

Finally, a calendar-related variable was constructed to detect the effects of organizational or other changes that might fall equally on old and young fleets. Without such a control, those calendar-based events could confound the measurement of age-related trends. To make the interpretation of the calendar coefficient and regression constant more easily understood, the calendar variable chosen was the relative number of years from 1998, the last year of the available data. Thus, a "year-1998" variable was constructed to detect and control for any net trends in on-equipment flightline workloads, so that we could avoid misinterpreting any of the changes listed near the end of Chapter Three as an effect of increasing aircraft age.

The main regression analysis first used these variables in an equation examining the combined effects of all terms. The full on-equipment regression equation is

$$W = (a * A) + (b * Y) + \sum_i (c_i * C_i) + \sum_j d_j M_j + \sum_k (e_k * B_k) +$$
$$(f * F) + (g * I) \qquad (4.5)$$

where

W = workload (dependent variable)

A = average age of aircraft fleet (FAge)

Y = years since 1998 (Year98)

C_i = categorical variables for command (AETC, AFE, PACAF, SOC, AMC, ANG, AFR)

M_j = categorical variables for mission (Bmbr, C2, Crgo, Helo, OSA, Tnkr, Trnr, U2)

B_k = break-in variables, where

B_1 = year 0 to 5 pulse variable

B_2 = year 0 to 10 pulse variable

B_3 = year 0 to 5 diminishing-ramp variable

B_4 = year 0 to 10 diminishing-ramp variable

F = flyaway cost of 100th aircraft in fleet (Flyaway)

i = command index variable

j = mission index variable

k = break-in variable index

I = interaction (cross product) of age and flyaway cost (FAge ∗ Fly), and a, b, c_i, d_j, e_k, f, and g are constants to be determined in the regression.

After reducing the equation to a minimum list of statistically significant variables whose probabilities of a zero coefficient were less than 5 percent, the study examined the potential for late-life workload acceleration or deceleration. To accomplish this, an additional second-order variable whose positive or negative coefficient would reflect acceleration or deceleration, respectively, was added to the reduced equation:

$$S = \left(A - 20 \right)^2 \qquad (4.6)$$

where

S = second-order age term (FAge20^2)

A = average age of aircraft fleet (FAge).

Thus, the second-order term was centered at age 20, near the midpoint of the available data. This value was chosen to minimize the correlation between age and the new term. While the two terms are not orthogonal, their correlation should be very low, minimizing the chance that they both measure the basic age effect.

The second-order term was not used in the full regression before the backward stepwise reduction, because the early-life break-in effects could create a significant effect that could be misconstrued as a second-order effect. This more-conservative approach would accept the second-order effect only if it added significantly to the reduced equation's explanatory power.

After the regression was performed, a preferred equation was identified. That equation and the associated data were then subjected to two tests, Cook's distance and leverage, to detect and identify any data that might have an undue influence on the regression results. *Cook's distance* is a measure of how much each observation influences the regression coefficients, including the intercept. *Leverage* measures how unusual an observation's independent (i.e., right-hand side) variables are, thus indicating the degree to which that point may be influential. Generally, points whose Cook's distance exceeds 1.0 and have high leverage compared with other points should be viewed with some suspicion.

If Cook's distance was larger than 1.0, its leverage was noted and a subsequent regression (including the stepwise backward reduction) was performed to measure the effects of the data points on both the coefficients and the stepwise retention of statistically significant terms. The consequences of those differences were examined in terms of the effects on age-related workload forecasts.

Finally, forecasts were developed for a notional $30-million fighter and a $100-million cargo aircraft. Those forecasts included an age-sensitive 95-percent error bound, in which the vast majority of actual workloads should fall (for the notional aircraft).

Off-Equipment (Component Repair) Data, Edits, and Regressions

The data for off-equipment component repair workloads were also obtained from REMIS PPS using a standard report. Two-digit WUC data were downloaded for each MDS and block in the second column of Table 4.3 for each command. No aircraft support general WUCs were observed in the data, so scheduled maintenance, unscheduled maintenance, and repair workloads were summed across the available WUCs and normalized by flying hours for each MDS and block, by command by year. As with the on-equipment data, records pertaining to AFMC activities, Foreign Military Sales, and non–Air Force activities were removed.

The control variables computed for on-equipment flightline workloads were also computed for off-equipment component repair, including the following:

1. Average fleet ages, based on the Air Force Program Data System (PDS) extract (FAge)

2. Four break-in variables, including two pulse variables (Pulse5 and Pulse10) and two diminishing-ramp (Ramp5 and Ramp10) variables

3. Basic mission categorical variables (Bmbr, C2, Crgo, Helo, ISR, Tnkr, Trnr)

4. Major command categorical variables (AETC, AFE, PACAF, SOC, AMC, ANG, AFR)

5. Flyaway cost (Flyaway)

6. Years since 1998 (Year98)

7. An age–flyaway cost interaction term (FAge*Fly).

Thus, the regression equation for off-equipment component repair workload was identical to the on-equipment flightline workload equation:

$$
W = \left(a * A\right) + \left(b * Y\right) + \sum_i c_i + C_i + \sum \left(d * M_j\right) + \sum_k \left(e_k * B_k\right) + \\
\left(f * F\right) + \left(g * I\right)
\tag{4.7}
$$

where all terms are as defined for Eq. (4.5).

As with the on-equipment analysis, this equation was reduced in a stepwise backward fashion until all remaining terms' probabilities of a zero coefficient were less than 5 percent. Then, a test was conducted for the presence of late-life acceleration or deceleration, as in the on-equipment (flightline) analysis. Tests were conducted to measure Cook's distance and leverage, and an alternative equation was developed if necessary. Finally, age-sensitive forecasts were developed for a $30-million fighter and a $100-million cargo aircraft.

Base Periodic-Inspection Data, Edits, and Regressions

When the REMIS PPS on-equipment flightline data were edited to remove periodic and special inspection workloads (WUC 03 and 04, respectively), those data were saved in another data file for subsequent analysis. The resultant data were found to be missing or substantially incomplete for calendar years 1994–1996. Only data for 1997 and 1998 were retained for analysis.

Further, insufficient isochronal (periodic inspections scheduled on a calendar basis, rather than phased inspections scheduled by consumed flying hours) inspection data were found for strategic airlift aircraft operated by the Air Mobility Command, including the C-5, C-17, and C-141. Likewise, only spotty data were found for Air National Guard or Air Force Reserve Command operating the same aircraft mission designs. Consequently, workload data for those aircraft were deleted from the analysis. Data were found in those commands for C-130 aircraft, and those data were retained.

No data for periodic or special inspections were found for any MDS operated by AFMC, Foreign Military Sales aircraft, or non–Air Force agencies.

The regression equations for base periodic inspection workloads were nearly identical to the on-equipment and off-equipment equations. The only difference was that the cargo mission area categorical variable was replaced by a C-130 mission area categorical variable, because the deletion of isochronal data affected mainly cargo aircraft.

Again, the full regression equation was reduced to a simpler equation, and a second-order term centered on age 20 was used in a post hoc test to detect any indications of late-life acceleration or deceleration effect. As with the other analyses, Cook's distance and leverage were computed for each observation, and an alternative equation was developed if necessary. Finally, age-related forecasts were developed for a $30-million fighter and a $100-million cargo aircraft.

Special Inspection Data, Edits, and Regressions

The special inspection analysis duplicated the phased inspection analysis in every respect except for the choice of dependent variable. Exactly the same aircraft and command records exhibited missing or underreported data in exactly the same years. Thus, the edits and regression equations, the Cook's distance, leverage tests, and the workload forecasts were conducted in exactly the same way.

Depot-Level Reparables Cost Data, Edits, and Regressions

RAND began archiving annual snapshots of the annual "scrubbed" March requirements data bank (RDB, originally AFMC's D041 database, replaced recently by D200) in 1993. (The RDB database changes constantly as material managers update factors associated with each component. Once a year, the managers review the data to ensure their accuracy and consistency. The result of that review is the annual "scrubbed" database, which becomes available in March each year.) Those data include recent consumption histories, flying hours, scrubbed estimates of current demand rates, repair costs and repair hours, and aircraft-component indenture relationships (that indicate which aircraft fleets have each component, and how many each has) for all master stock numbers in the Air Force DLR inventory. The Air Force uses these factors to estimate near-term DLR repair demands and budget requirements. This database is not ideal for this analysis, because individual DLR demands are not recorded against each aircraft MDS in D041 or D200. Instead, the system simply adds up all the demands across all weapon systems for each master stock number, and then implicitly allocates the demands for shared components by assuming all aircraft generate the same number of demands per component flying hour. Fortunately for this study, demands and repair costs for components that are not shared across aircraft are accurately attributed to those aircraft.

As a further complication, the D041/D200 aggregation process also obscures how many demands each command experienced for each part. Thus, it is not possible to detect or measure any cross-command differences in consumption.

D041/D200 records both the current year's maintenance prices and labor standards (i.e., expected labor hours to repair) for each part.

Beginning in 1993, with the establishment of DLR pricing, the frequency of records with nonblank labor standards has increased steadily. Although it implies that the quality of those data is increasing, labor-hour standards cannot be compared meaningfully across multiple years. Thus, the study used the repair price rather than labor hours to reflect workload.

The consumption rates for most aircraft components are recorded in terms of the number of demands per flying hour. Only those components so recorded were used. Since the individual component data are too varied and sparse to indicate any general effects of aging aircraft, we computed the cost of repairing components for a single flying hour for each MDS to obtain a more understandable measure, using the following formula:

$$D_m = \sum_{\ell \text{ in MDS}} \left(O_\ell * Q_{\ell m} * P_{\ell m} * N_\ell * R_\ell \right) \qquad (4.8)$$

where

D_m = cost of repairing components for MDS m

ℓ = index to components

m = index to mission design series

O_ℓ = operations and intermediate demands for depot-level repair of component ℓ per flying hour, expressed in D041/D200 as a fraction of a demand per hundred flying hours

$Q_{\ell m}$ = quantity of the item installed on aircraft

$P_{\ell m}$ = fraction of aircraft MDS m that use item ℓ

N_ℓ = worldwide fraction of O_ℓ that are not reparable at a base or intermediate facility

R_ℓ = price to repair one component ℓ at a depot repair facility or contractor.

Summed, this equation estimates the repair expenditures a fleet would require per flying hour in a particular year.

Of course, this value is the price charged by the Depot Maintenance Activity Group (DMAG) to the Supply Management Activity Group (SMAG) that year. It should be distinguished from the exchange price (which includes an allocated cost for operating the material management, storage, and distribution functions of the SMAG) plus the cost of buying new DLRs charged to the using unit. (The cost of buying new DLRs is discussed separately below.) The value in Eq. (4.8) should also be distinguished from the actual average cost of repairing those components in the target year. It is, instead, the price charged based on actual costs from recent repair experience. As such, it is a lagging indicator of the actual cost, predicted from the previous two years' histories and used to predict budgets two years after the year when the data are scrubbed.

All price data were adjusted to constant FY98 dollars using the AF-CAIG O&M inflation factors for each year from AFI 65-503, Attachment A45-1 (USAF, SAF/FMC, 1998).

The data were edited to remove MDS whose DLR coverage was known to be incomplete. Several fleets, including the various reconnaissance platforms (e.g., U-2, RC-135) have classified systems whose components are managed outside D041/D200. Likewise, the F-117, the KC-10, and most operations support aircraft (e.g., C-12, C-26) receive most of their component repair services under a contractor logistics support arrangement. Those aircraft were excluded from the analysis so that their abnormally low demands would not bias any analysis of the age effect. Several small, special-purpose fleets (e.g., LC-130, WC-130, NKC-135) were also excluded because their atypical missions may affect demands for reasons unrelated to age.

Because the D041/D200 data are aggregated across commands, the command categorical variables were not available for the analysis. However, the other control variables used in the on-equipment and off-equipment analyses were available:

1. Average fleet ages, based on the Air Force PDS extract

2. Four break-in variables

3. Basic mission category variables

4. Flyaway cost

5. Years since 1998

6. The age–flyaway cost interaction variable.

Thus, the regression equation for DLR repair costs was slightly simpler than the equation for on-equipment, off-equipment, phased inspection, or special inspection workloads:

$$D = (a * A) + (b * Y) + \sum_j d_j M_j + \sum_k (e_k * B_k) + $$
$$(f * F) + (g * I) \tag{4.9}$$

where all terms are as defined for Eq. (4.5).

As with the previous analyses, the equation was reduced in a stepwise backward fashion until all remaining terms' probabilities of a zero coefficient were less than 5 percent. Likewise, a second-order term centered on 20 years was used in a post hoc analysis to detect any indication of late-life acceleration or deceleration. Cook's distance and leverage were computed for every observation and an alternative equation was developed if necessary. Age-related forecasts were developed for a $30-million fighter and a $100-million cargo aircraft.

General Stock Division (GSD) Material Cost Data, Edits, and Regressions

The data for GSD material consumption were obtained from the 1999 and 2001 editions of the annual AFCAIG O&M Planning Factors, AFI 65-503 Attachment 2-1 (USAF, AFCAIG, 1998b, 2000a). The GSD planning factors are organized by MDS and are normalized by flying hours across all commands. As with the DLR repair-costs data, the GSD data were adjusted to constant 1998 dollars using the AFCAIG O&M Attachment A49-1 inflation factors.

Again, the command categorical variables were not available for analysis, so the simpler regression (Eq. [4.9] above) used in DLR repair was also used to analyze GSD consumption patterns. After the full regression was examined, it was reduced in a stepwise fashion until all remaining terms' probabilities of a zero coefficient were less than 5 percent. As with the previous analyses, a second-order term centered on age 20 was used in a post hoc analysis to detect any indication of late-life acceleration or deceleration. Again, Cook's distance and leverage were computed, and forecasts were developed for notional aircraft.

Support Equipment Purchase Data, Edits, and Regressions

The data for support equipment purchases were also obtained from the 1999 and 2001 editions of AFI 65-503 Attachment 2-1 (USAF, AF-CAIG, 1998b, 2000a). Those factors are also organized by MDS, but they are normalized by Primary Authorized Aircraft instead of by flying hour. As with the DLR and GSD data, the support equipment purchased data were adjusted to constant 1998 dollars using the AF-CAIG O&M inflation factors.

The command categorical variables were not available; therefore, this analysis used the simpler DLR regression (Eq. [4.9]) to analyze the support equipment purchase life-cycle pattern. After the full regression was completed, it was reduced in a stepwise fashion until all remaining terms' probabilities of a zero coefficient were less than 5 percent. A second-order term centered on age 20 was added to both reduced equations in a post hoc analysis to detect the presence of any late-life acceleration or deceleration. Cook's distance and leverage were computed. Forecasts were developed for a $30-million fighter and a $100-million cargo aircraft.

Programmed Depot Maintenance (PDM) Workload Data, Edits, and Regressions

PDM workload data are not archived by the Air Force. However, hardcopy files maintained in several System Program Directors' (SPDs') offices were provided for this analysis. Those data were complemented with data recorded during previous Project AIR FORCE studies (Marks and Hess, 1981; Paulson and Hoffmayer, 1980).

PDM data were provided in various forms, with differing content. In all cases, the workload data were the results of the Material Requirements Review Board (MRRB) negotiations for the stated year. Those annual negotiations among the using major operating command, the SPD, and the performing maintenance organization determine the list of tasks to be performed and the labor hours allocated to each task for PDMs to be performed in a target year. They are based in large measure on reviews of work performed on similar aircraft during the previous three years, and they determine the planned work for PDMs three years in the future. For example, the MRRB negotiations that occur in spring 2003 will draw on previous PDM workloads from FY2000 through FY2002 to determine planned work for FY2006.

Those workload forecasts are subsequently used by the major operating command to develop its budget requests for the target year. Once those funding programs are proposed (two years before the target year), the MRRB generally permits only limited adjustments to the planned PDM workload, especially the total.

The negotiations for all aircraft with the same basic MD (e.g., various versions of the C-130) occur at the same MRRB meeting. Thus, experiences with older MDS are used to indicate what future work may arise on younger MDS (e.g., C-130E experience will identify work that may be needed on C-130H aircraft). If that work was discovered relatively late with the older MDS, the younger MDS MRRB workloads may incorporate it earlier.

The C-135 SPD provided the most-comprehensive data, which distinguished tanker workloads from other C-135 aircraft, separated planned workload from over-and-above workload (unprogrammed repair work discovered during the PDM), and covered the period beginning in 1980 and ending in 1998. Those data also separated modification workloads from standard inspection and repair workloads.

The F-15, C-130, and C-5 SPDs provided historical data for a shorter period at the MDS level of detail, beginning in 1990. They comprised only the planned workloads, including TCTOs, through 1998. Data for the C-130 were further disaggregated by production-run blocks (e.g., 1977–1979 C-130H models versus later C-130Hs). PDM workload data were also obtained from 1997 and 1998 MRRB documents for the B-52 and C-141, at the MDS level of detail. Finally, PDM workload data were obtained from previous RAND research for the B-52, C-130, C-5, C-135, and C141 in 1977 and 1979. The 1977 data provided C-5 PDM workloads with and without a modification workload then in progress.

To make the data more nearly commensurate with each other, over-and-above data (available only for the C-135) were removed from the analysis, and TCTO workload data from the REMIS GSCAS were used to remove TCTO (modification) workloads from the C-5, C-130, and F-15 data. The 1977 C-5A data point that excluded the modification workload was selected.

With the exception of the 1977 and 1979 data, the resulting data reflected MRRB-approved PDM workloads for the aircraft entering that process each year. The data were not time- or age-compensated to adjust for the lag between data collection and the approval date.

Because information about older aircraft workloads is used to adjust younger aircraft workloads, two new variables were constructed, one to measure the average age of the lead fleet (MDS) for each mission design, and another to measure the offset between the target fleet's average age and the associated lead-fleet age. Thus, it was possible to detect and measure the extent to which the PDM workloads for younger fleets may exceed those for the oldest fleet as a result of the earlier introduction of some work in the younger fleets, as in the C-130E and C-130H example described above.

We obtained data specifying the inspection interval for each MDS from Air Force Technical Order (AFTO) 00-25-4 (U.S. Air Force, 1999). When different intervals were specified for different portions of a single fleet, the largest subfleet's interval was used. For example, KC-135s assigned to the Pacific Air Command have a shorter PDM interval than the rest of the fleet has, but they are also a far smaller fleet, so the longer interval (60 months) was chosen for this analysis.

The small number of fleets with available PDM data and the dominance of cargo aircraft in the sample made any analysis of differences by basic mission impractical. Thus, categorical variables were not developed for basic mission types but were developed for each MD.

Finally, the Air Force implemented several changes in its PDM program after 1992, including changing the funding mechanism to create a buyer-seller relationship between the commands and each

PDM shop. To capture changes resulting from that change, an additional variable, Z, was created to detect and measure any post-1992 trends in workload that may be due to factors other than age:

$$Z = \begin{cases} \text{Year} - 1992 & \text{Year} \geq 1992 \\ 0 & \text{otherwise} \end{cases} \tag{4.10}$$

Again, data were not available by command, so the full regression equation is

$$W = \sum \left(e_k * B_k\right) + \left(f * F\right) + \left(g * L\right) + \left(h * G\right) + \left(p * P\right) +$$
$$\sum_m \left(q_m + Q_m\right) + \left(r * Z\right) + \left(s * L * F\right) + \left(t * G * F\right) \tag{4.11}$$

where

Z = years greater than 1992 (Year92)

L = lead fleet age (LdAge)

G = years subject fleet follows lead fleet (Follow)

   $= L - A$

P = inter-PDM interval (Period)

Q_m = MDS categorical variables (B52, C5, C130, C135, C141)

$e_k, f, g, h, p, q_m, r, s,$ and t are constant coefficients to be determined.

Other variables are as defined in Eqs. (4.5) through (4.9), except that the lead fleet age was used in place of the average fleet age throughout. Thus, the four break-in terms and the second-order age term were recomputed using lead fleet age instead of average fleet age. Thus, those terms were computed as

B_1 = 5-year PDM pulse variable (LPulse5)

$$= \begin{cases} 1 & 0 \le L \le 5 \\ 0 & \text{otherwise} \end{cases} \tag{4.12}$$

B_2 = 10-year PDM pulse variable (LPulse10)

$$= \begin{cases} 1 & 0 \le L \le 10 \\ 0 & \text{otherwise} \end{cases} \tag{4.13}$$

B_3 = 5-year PDM ramp variable (LRamp5)

$$= \begin{cases} \dfrac{5-L}{5} & 0 \le L \le 5 \\ 0 & \text{otherwise} \end{cases} \tag{4.14}$$

B_4 = 10-year PDM ramp variable (LRamp10)

$$= \begin{cases} \dfrac{10-L}{10} & 0 \le L \le 10 \\ 0 & \text{otherwise} \end{cases} \tag{4.15}$$

The second-order age term was likewise adjusted to be

$$S = \text{second-order PDM age term (LdAge20}^2) = (20 - L)^2 \tag{4.16}$$

After the full regression was completed, it was reduced in a stepwise backward fashion until all remaining terms' probabilities of a zero coefficient were less than 5 percent. In a post hoc analysis, a second-order term centered on age 20 was added to the reduced equation to detect the presence of any late-life acceleration or deceleration. Cook's distance and leverage were computed. Forecasts were developed for a $30-million fighter and a $100-million cargo aircraft.

Depot Engine Workload Data, Edits, and Regressions

We obtained engine overhaul data from two sources, the 1999 *Engine Handbook* (USAF, SA-ALC, 1999a) and the FY99/00 Engine Overhaul

Depot Product Standard Hours Workload (USAF, SA-ALC, 1999b). The first source provided the average time between overhauls, expressed in engine flying hours, the engine weight, whether it was a fan engine, whether it had a scheduled overhaul, and whether it used an augmentor. The second provided the labor hours planned in FY99 and FY00 to overhaul some engines at the depot.

Engine overhaul labor per engine flying hour was computed as

$$W = \frac{\text{DPSH}}{\text{ATBO}} \tag{4.17}$$

where

DPSH = depot product standard hours per engine overhaul

ATBO = average engine flying hours between overhauls.

Categorical variables were developed to distinguish some high-performance turbofan engines from others, to distinguish augmented (fighter) engines from others, to distinguish between engines with and without scheduled overhauls, and to distinguish the F110 engine and the F100 engine variants from other augmented engines. Thus, overhaul characteristics unique to either of those two widely employed engines could be distinguished from those of other augmented engines.

Engine average age was computed as the average of the time since the military qualification time (MQT) and the time since last purchase. No engine's average fleet age was less than six years, so we computed only the 10-year break-in variables. The resulting regression equation is

$$W = b + Y + \left(u * E\right) + \left(v * R\right) + \left(w * C\right) + \left(x * E\right) + \left(y * N\right) +$$
$$\sum_{\ell}\left(a_\ell * F_\ell\right) + \sum_{k=3}^{4} e_k B_k + \left(g * E * R\right) \tag{4.18}$$

where

E = engine average age (EAge)

R = engine weight (EWeight)

C = categorical variable for turbofan engine (Fan)

E = categorical variable for augmented engine (Aug)

N = categorical variable for no engine overhaul (NoOH)

F_ℓ = categorical variables for F100 and F110 engines (F100 and F110)

and $b, u, v, w, x, y, a_\ell, e_k,$ and g are constants to be determined.

Other variables are as defined in Eqs. (4.3) through (4.18), except that the engine age was used in place of the average fleet age throughout. Thus, the four break-in variables and the second-order age term were recomputed using average engine age instead of average fleet age. Those terms were computed as

B_1 = 5-year engine pulse variable (EPulse5)

$$= \begin{cases} 1 & 0 \leq E \leq 5 \\ 0 & \text{otherwise} \end{cases} \tag{4.19}$$

B_2 = 10-year engine pulse variable (EPulse10)

$$= \begin{cases} 1 & 0 \leq E \leq 10 \\ 0 & \text{otherwise} \end{cases} \tag{4.20}$$

B_3 = 5-year engine ramp variable (ERamp5)

$$= \begin{cases} \dfrac{5 - E}{5} & 0 \leq E \leq 5 \\ 0 & \text{otherwise} \end{cases} \tag{4.21}$$

B_4 = 10-year engine ramp variable (ERamp10)

$$= \begin{cases} \dfrac{10 - E}{10} & 0 \le E \le 10 \\ 0 & \text{otherwise} \end{cases} \qquad (4.22)$$

Likewise, the second-order term became

$S=$ second-order engine age term $(\text{EAge20}^2) = (E - 20)^2$ \qquad (4.23)

Once the full regression was completed, it was reduced in a stepwise fashion until all remaining terms' probabilities of a zero coefficient were less than 5 percent. A second-order term centered on age 20 was added post hoc to detect the presence of any late-life acceleration or deceleration. Cook's distance and leverage were computed. Overhaul workload forecasts were developed for a 3,700-lb fighter engine and a 5,000-lb cargo engine.

Per-Aircraft Contractor Logistics Support Cost Data, Edits, and Regressions

AFCAIG reports two additional factors for contractor logistics support (CLS) in AFI 65-503, Attachment 6-1 (USAF, 1998a, 2000b). The data from 1999 and 2001 were used in this analysis. As before, average ages were obtained from the Air Force PDS.

The two factors represent two different components of aircraft costs, as they appear in CLS contracts. The first component is a fixed cost associated with keeping the aircraft operational in the USAF inventory. It is priced on a "per-aircraft" basis, and we have called it the "per-aircraft CLS cost." The second component is a variable cost of operations associated with the additional maintenance required to restore material failures induced by operational flying activity. It is priced on a "per-flying-hour" basis. CLS aircraft may require either or both kinds of support. In this subsection, we discuss the analysis for the per-aircraft-CLS cost.

In contrast to previous analyses cited in this study, we developed a categorical variable to detect any differences between 1999 and 2001 data. We did so because initial regressions indicated an unbelievably high rate of cost increase between those two years. We were unable to identify an operational or accounting-factor change to explain the very large change, so we used a categorical variable to avoid misinterpreting the shift as a trend.

Again, the data were not disaggregated by command, so we developed no command categorical data. In addition, no basic mission data were developed, because cargo aircraft and their derivatives dominated the available data. Thus, the full regression equation for this analysis is

$$D = jY_{99} + (a*A) + \sum_k (e_k * B_k) + (f*F) + (g*I) \qquad (4.24)$$

where

$$Y_{99} = \begin{cases} 1 & \text{if the year is 1999 (Year99)} \\ 0 & \text{otherwise} \end{cases} \qquad (4.25)$$

Other variables are as defined for Eqs. (4.5) through (4.23).

Once the full regression was completed, it was reduced in a stepwise backward fashion until all remaining terms' probabilities of a zero coefficient were less than 5 percent. We added a second-order term centered on age 20 post hoc to detect the presence of any late-life acceleration or deceleration. Cook's distance and leverage were computed. Forecasts were developed for a $30-million fighter and a $100-million cargo aircraft.

Per-Flying-Hour CLS Cost Data, Edits, and Regressions

As with the per-aircraft CLS cost data, we obtained the per-flying-hour data from the 1999 and 2001 editions of AFI 65-503, Attachment 6-1 (USAF, AFCAIG, 1998a, 2000b). The analysis approach was identical to that for per-aircraft data, except that there were far fewer entries (only 20 total) in the attachments. The full regression equation was identical to Eq. (4.25) above.

Once the full regression was completed, it was reduced in a stepwise backward fashion until all remaining terms' probabilities of a zero coefficient was less than 5 percent. We added a second-order term centered on age 20 post hoc to detect the presence of any late-life acceleration or deceleration. Cook's distance and leverage were computed. Forecasts were developed for a $30-million fighter and a $100-million cargo aircraft.

Depot-Level Reparables Purchase Data, Edits, and Regressions

DLR procurement data for several sequential years were acquired from a RAND researcher's personal archive of the USAF portion of the Presidential Budget submissions from 1994 through 1999 (USAF, 1994–1999). Those data were available only at the MD level of detail, so it is possible that some age-related DLR procurement-cost growth may be underestimated.

Those data were gross annual expenditures for each aircraft fleet, so they were normalized by total aircraft inventory for the regression analysis. Again, data were not available by command, so no command categorical data were developed. Thus, the regression equations duplicate the equations for the DLR repair analysis, Eq. (4.9).

Once the full regression equation was completed, we reduced it in a stepwise backward fashion until all remaining terms' probabilities of a zero coefficient were less than 5 percent. We then added a second-order term centered on age 20 to detect the presence of any late-life acceleration or deceleration. Cook's distance and leverage were computed. Forecasts were developed for a $30-million fighter and a $100-million cargo aircraft.

Historical Modification Workloads Data, Edits, and Regressions

REMIS GSCAS collects and maintains extensive data about modifications—planned, underway, and accomplished. It maintains configuration-control information about individual USAF aircraft and historical workload information about every TCTO authorized for each MDS, including when it was issued and rescinded, what organization was authorized to perform it, and how much effort was planned per aircraft. Thus, the Air Force has a comprehensive history of the planned labor associated with modifications. But it has no history of the actual labor expended.

Additional Independent Variables from Other USAF Data Sources. TCTO workloads depend not on an individual aircraft's age, but on the age of the design and the need to update that design. Thus, it is possible that a relatively young aircraft may require a modification because its design is outdated. In view of this observation, we used the aircraft fleet's design age in the analysis of TCTO workloads. Therefore, two aircraft sharing the same basic mission design (MD) designation (e.g., an F-15A and an F-15C) would have the same mission design age, because their basic designs share so many common characteristics. In that case, the modification (and TCTO labor requirements) needed to update those common characteristics might occur about the same design age, not the same fleet age. To compute the design age, we used the age of the oldest tail number in the current MD, as maintained in the Air Force Program Data System.

Although the previous design horizons may have been about 20 years, other surprise requirements may emerge that cause USAF decisionmakers to upgrade USAF aircraft more frequently. Operating on the hypothesis that an aircraft has a design horizon, after which time it will require a substantial modification to ensure its continued usefulness, we added a series of 5-year-long "upgrade pulses" to the regression. We included a categorical variable for each 5-year design-age interval, starting at age 10–15. The variables were constructed to be nonoverlapping intervals. For example, the "20–25" interval was constructed to be greater than or equal to 20 and less than (but not equal to) 25. Note that the large window for each variable will also dampen the measured size of any individual large modification, because it will be averaged with smaller modifications in surrounding years. That is, the TCTO regression will almost certainly underestimate the peak size of the modification workload, even if it detects a change within the window. The estimated size will be the average deviation during that time, effectively estimating the major-modification effect as though it were spread over the entire 5-year window.

Once again, the data were not disaggregated by command, so we developed no command categorical data. However, basic mission data were available. The full regression equation for this analysis is

$$W = \left(z*U\right) + \sum_{j}\left(d_j*M_j\right) + \sum_{k}\left(e_k*B_k\right) + \left(f*F\right) +$$
$$\left(g*I\right) + \sum_{\ell}\left(v_\ell*V_\ell\right) \qquad (4.26)$$

where

U = age of design (DAge)

$$V_\ell = \begin{cases} 1 & 5+5\ell \leq U \leq 10+5\ell, \; \ell = 1, 2, 3, 4, 5, 6 \\ & \qquad \text{(D10, D15, D20, D25, D30, D35)} \;\; (4.27) \\ 0 & \text{otherwise} \end{cases}$$

where z and V_ℓ are constants to be determined and all other variables are as defined in Eqs. (4.5) through (4.23).

Once the full regression was completed, we reduced it in a stepwise backward fashion until all remaining terms' probabilities of a zero coefficient were less than 5 percent. We then added a second-order term centered on age 20 to detect the presence of any late-life deceleration or acceleration. Cook's distance and leverage were computed, and alternative equations were developed if necessary. Forecasts were developed for a $30-million fighter and a $100-million cargo aircraft.

Chapter Five

AGE-RELATED WORKLOAD AND MATERIAL COST GROWTH: FINDINGS

We now turn to the relationships between aircraft age and workload or material consumption yielded by the equations described in Chapter Four. The relationship of greatest interest is how fleets' workloads and material consumption patterns may grow in later life, so that extrapolations can be made more confidently to ages past those already experienced. As discussed in Chapters Two and Three, many factors that may affect workloads and material consumption in early life may be absent later in life. Also, exogenous factors unrelated to age may also affect workloads and material consumption. Therefore, we had to control for the early-life transitions and known exogenous events that may obscure or exaggerate later-life growth in the available historical record.

SUMMARY OF FINDINGS

Six major points are drawn from the analyses:

- Most maintenance workloads grow as fleets age.

- More-expensive aircraft often have faster-growing workloads and material consumption rates.

- GSD material consumption growth decelerates as aircraft age.

- PDM workload growth accelerates in the third and fourth decades of service.

- Modification workloads do not grow, but they surge about age 20.
- Other processes may hide or exaggerate age-related effects.

Each point is discussed in turn in the remainder of this summary.

Most Aircraft Maintenance Workloads Grow as Fleets Age, Although at Varying Rates

Most, but not all, USAF maintenance workloads and material consumption categories grow as aircraft age. The only exception was the periodic inspection workloads. With that exception, workloads grow as fleets age, regardless of whether maintenance is performed on- or off-aircraft or located at the base or the depot. Maintenance material consumption also grows whether it is consumable GSD bits and pieces, depot-level reparables, or whole support equipment.

More-Expensive Aircraft Often Have Faster-Growing Workloads and Material Consumption Rates

That growth is not uniform across fleets or workloads. Some workloads, such as fighter intermediate maintenance, grow very slowly—about 18 maintenance manhours per year for a $30-million fighter flying 300 hours per year. Others grow more rapidly, such as cargo-aircraft PDM—about 1,700 manhours per year for a 40-year-old $100-million cargo aircraft.

This study found that the key factor affecting growth rate for each workload was the flyaway cost of the aircraft. In most cases, the growth rate was proportional to the aircraft flyaway cost. Thus, a $100-million cargo aircraft's intermediate maintenance would grow 60 maintenance manhours per year (compared with the $30-million fighter's 18 manhours). The PDM workload also grows more quickly for more-expensive aircraft, but the growth is not proportional to the flyaway cost. Thus, a $200-million cargo aircraft's PDM would grow about 2,500 hours per year at age 40, far less than twice the PDM growth for the $100-million cargo aircraft.

GSD Material Consumption Growth Decelerates as Aircraft Age

The hypothesis that there must be some limit to the various workloads that would cause the ultimate sizes of workload growth to decelerate in very late life was not confirmed, except for the GSD material-consumption category. At least for the service lives and technologies observed in this analysis, we found no evidence that any maintenance workload growth decelerated in later life.

The GSD regression results indicate consumption would actually begin to decline after 20–40 years, depending on aircraft flyaway cost. That may only reflect a late-life leveling off of consumption because of the limited data available. If so, future analyses of GSD material consumption with more extended historical data will develop more-reliable long-term forecasts with less statistical uncertainty at ages past 50 years.

PDM Workload Growth Accelerates in the Third and Fourth Decades of Service

Although this study found that the GSD material consumption decelerates, it also found that the PDM workload accelerates. Unlike any other workload or material consumption category, the PDM workload grows at an increasingly rapid rate as the aircraft fleets age. While a $100-million cargo aircraft's workload grows about 1,150 hours per year when it is age 20 years, it grows about 1,700 hours per year when it is age 40 years.

This difference may partially confirm the hypothesis advanced in Chapter Three that major structural maintenance (both inspections and repairs) will initially accelerate as an aircraft approaches and surpasses its original design life, then decelerate as some workload limit is reached. Given the fleet histories currently available, we have been able to confirm the acceleration part of that hypothesis, but not the subsequent deceleration. Again, more data from more aged fleets will test that hypothesis over time.

Modification Workloads Do Not Grow, but They Surge About Age 20

As for the base periodic inspection workload, we found no growth in depot and contractor modification workloads. In fact, we found that the B-2A data very strongly influenced the regression and that removing those data yielded an equation in which the normal (nonsurge) workload steadily declined.

One interpretation of this downward trend is that modification investments may decline as the Air Force strives to ensure that the newest MD or MDS within a mission area stays at the cutting edge of the technological state of the art until it is superseded by a new design. After that, the available modification budgets may shift to the latest MD or MDS. If so, we may find that the TCTO workload pattern generally declines for existing platforms.

Although that downward trend was unexpected, the age 20–25 surge observed in both regressions matched the expected design-horizon effect suggested in Chapter Three. However, a closer review of the underlying data found that the surges occur much more randomly across aircraft and times, and are much larger than indicated in the regression equation parameter. Almost all aircraft may require a large mid-life modification; however, the actual timing of that upgrade may depend on a number of other factors, including the availability of funds and the competing needs of other aircraft platforms. The planning, programming, and budgeting decisions that shift modification funding to the most-pressing Air Force requirements may have moved some modifications into adjacent periods, both reducing the estimated size of the surge and reducing the overall explanatory power of the regression.

Other Processes May Hide or Exaggerate Age-Related Effects

Processes other than long-term material deterioration affect maintenance workloads and material consumption patterns over time. Our analyses found MAJCOM differences, 20–25-year workload surges, cross-MDS learning, and different break-in effects—all of which could have obscured or exaggerated the age relationship.

Early-life transitions pose particularly troublesome problems for those who would predict later-life workload growth. Some workloads experience honeymoon periods; others experience initial transient peaks. No matter which pattern emerges in early life, it will exaggerate or obscure analysts' attempts to measure long-term, late-life growth. Because the underlying causes for growth in the two periods are different, anyone wishing to forecast later-life workloads must discount the early-life effects. Moreover, forecasts of workloads for future fleets and fleets currently being fielded should also reflect those early-life patterns and the transitions to later-life growth.

We now turn to a detailed description of the findings for each of the 13 categories for which we found data.

FINDINGS FOR ON-EQUIPMENT (FLIGHTLINE) WORKLOADS

Table 5.1 shows the parameter coefficient estimates for the full regression of on-equipment workloads as aircraft fleets age. As discussed in Chapter Four, categorical variables were included for operating command, basic platform mission, aircraft fleets with an average age less than five years, and fleets younger than ten years. Continuous variables were included for aircraft flyaway cost, average fleet age, the fraction of the first five years remaining, the fraction of the first ten years remaining, and the interaction (product) of age and flyaway cost. Also discussed in Chapter Four, fighter aircraft in the Air Combat Command (ACC) were used as the reference set for the categorical variables.

The coefficients represent additive differences. For example, they imply that cargo aircraft (Crgo) generally require 3.2 additional maintenance manhours per flying hour than do fighter aircraft. Likewise, tankers (Tnkrs) and trainers (Trnrs) require 8.2 and 4.5 fewer maintenance manhours per flying hour, respectively, than do fighters.

The probabilities in the rightmost column of the table are computed from the t-statistic immediately adjacent. They represent the probability that the coefficient estimated in the first column is not really zero. (The t-statistic is computed as the ratio between the first two columns, which are the coefficient estimate and its standard error.)

Thus, in Table 5.1, we can see that only the cargo, tanker, trainer, electronic command and control (C2), Air Force Reserve, Air Mobility Command, Air National Guard, the flyaway cost, the interaction between flyaway cost and age, and the 5-year break-in ramp

Table 5.1

Age and Cost Affect On-Equipment Workloads in the Full Regression

Results of regression analysis
Analysis Performed: Sun 03 Mar 2002 15:28:44
Data set used: D:\Documents\Dbases\Analysis\DataFiles\OnEq
Rule set used: D:\Documents\Dbases\Analysis\Rules\OnEq2

Dependent variable:	LWork			
Total sum of squares	7.8732E+04			
Regression sum of squares	5.3991E+04			
Residual error	2.4741E+04			
F-Statistic	43.6444			
Degrees of freedom	21,420			
R-squared	0.6858			

Variable	Coefficient	Standard Error	t-Statistic	Probability
Constant	6.1931			
Bmbr	−1.1101	3.3774	−0.3287	0.7418
C2	−13.6056	1.9984	−6.8082	6.61E-07
Crgo	3.2342	1.4339	2.2556	0.0231
Tnkr	−8.1574	2.0076	−4.0633	1.98E-04
Trnr	−4.4639	2.2070	−2.0226	0.0411
U2	4.5722	2.7498	1.6627	0.0931
AETC	1.0677	1.4015	0.7619	0.5470
AFE	1.50E-03	1.4966	1.00E-03	0.9944
AFR	5.4300	1.3796	3.9358	2.74E-04
AMC	−7.9098	1.8541	−4.2661	1.20E-04
ANG	6.7685	1.1665	5.8022	4.14E-06
PAF	2.0069	1.3033	1.5399	0.1202
SOC	6.1779	3.6996	1.6699	0.0916
Flyaway	0.0410	0.0057	7.1906	3.51E-07
Year98	0.3988	0.2665	1.4963	0.1313
FAge	0.0425	0.0902	0.4712	0.6431
FAge*Fly	0.0069	6.20E-04	11.1645	2.20E-09
Pulse5	−2.9353	3.0183	−0.9725	0.6673
Pulse10	1.0677	1.7866	0.5976	0.5577
Ramp5	23.4247	7.0483	3.3234	1.35E-03
Ramp10	−6.0158	5.3260	−1.1295	0.2581

variables have probabilities less than 0.05, indicating a high probability that those variables actually affect the workload, and that the others may not. For example, the cargo aircraft coefficient discussed above probably reflects real differences between fighters and cargo aircraft flightline workloads, but the larger U2 coefficient is much less likely to reflect a real difference (i.e., after we account for the difference in flyaway costs and age).

The nonsignificant regression variables were eliminated progressively through a stepwise backward regression. In that process, the least-significant variable was removed from the full equation, then the regression was reestimated and the probabilities of the remaining coefficients were examined. Variables were removed one at a time in this iterative manner until all coefficients had probabilities of .05 or less. The final results from that process are displayed in Table 5.2.

We can see that all the variables that were statistically significant in the initial full regression remained significant in the reduced equation. In fact, one nonsignificant variable in the full regression— Ramp10, the 10-year break-in ramp—emerged as significant in the reduced equation. Its emergence is probably due to the removal of other variables that were highly correlated. That the 10-year break-in ramp variable emerged as significant counteracts the already-significant 5-year ramp variable, implying the presence of a 5-year infantile-failure process and a 10-year honeymoon process.

No Deceleration Was Detected in On-Equipment Workloads

As shown in Table 5.3, the regression found no evidence that on-equipment workloads accelerate or decelerate in late-life, because the $FAge20^2$ factor in that table was not significant at the .05 level when added to the reduced equation. We next examined more closely the linear equation whose parameters are shown in Table 5.2 to understand the practical implications for future USAF fleets (see the following subsection).

But first, to determine whether any point may have an undue influence on the results, we examined the Cook's distance and leverage values in a scatterplot. In this regression, all data points were within acceptable levels for Cook's distance, even those points near the high

Table 5.2

Age and Cost Interact to Affect On-Equipment Workloads
in the Reduced Regression

Results of regression analysis
Analysis Performed: Sun 03 Mar 2002 15:39:51
Data set used: D:\Documents\Dbases\Analysis\DataFiles\OnEq
Rule set used: D:\Documents\Dbases\Analysis\Rules\OnEq2

Dependent variable:	LWork
Total sum of squares	7.8732E+04
Regression sum of squares	5.3338E+04
Residual error	2.5394E+04
F-Statistic	82.1055
Degrees of freedom	11,430
R-squared	0.6775

Variable	Coefficient	Standard Error	t-Statistic	Probability
Constant	7.3095			
C2	−13.1560	1.8026	−7.2985	2.94E-07
Crgo	4.2036	1.0687	3.9333	2.75E-04
Tnkr	−7.4238	1.3021	−5.7016	5.03E-06
Trnr	−4.5321	1.6486	−2.7492	0.0063
AFR	4.3184	1.2136	3.5582	7.25E-04
AMC	−9.0670	1.6271	−5.5726	6.51E-06
ANG	5.8339	0.9904	5.8907	3.47E-06
Flyaway	0.0407	4.18E-03	9.7446	1.03E-08
FAge*Fly	0.0067	5.63E-04	11.8796	1.07E-09
Ramp5	18.5080	5.2901	3.4986	8.49E-04
Ramp10	−7.4788	2.9215	−2.5599	0.0105

end of the leverage scale. Thus, there is no evidence that any single
data point or small subset of data points had undue influence on the
results.

Practical Implications of the Reduced On-Equipment Regression Equation

The remainder of this subsection explores the life cycle on-equipment workload patterns detected in the reduced regression equation
for both a $30-million fighter and a $100-million cargo aircraft.

Figure 5.1 displays the computed per-flying-hour expected-value on-
equipment workload forecasts for $30-million fighter and $100-

Table 5.3

On-Equipment Workloads Do Not Decelerate

Results of regression analysis
Analysis Performed: Sun 03 Mar 2002 15:41:47
Data set used: D:\Documents\Dbases\Analysis\DataFiles\OnEq
Rule set used: D:\Documents\Dbases\Analysis\Rules\OnEq2

Dependent variable:	LWork
Total sum of squares	7.8732E+04
Regression sum of squares	5.3367E+04
Residual error	2.5365E+04
F-Statistic	75.2180
Degrees of freedom	12,429
R-squared	0.6778

Variable	Coefficient	Standard Error	t-Statistic	Probability
Constant	7.7031			
C2	–13.2429	1.8078	–7.3255	2.82E-07
Crgo	4.5637	1.1841	3.8542	3.36E-04
Tnkr	6.1066	2.2707	–2.6893	0.0074
Trnr	–4.1246	1.7470	–2.3610	0.0177
AFR	4.3206	1.2143	3.5580	7.26E-04
AMC	–9.3686	1.6828	–5.5673	6.59E-06
ANG	5.7994	0.9921	5.8453	3.79E-06
Flyaway	0.0409	4.19E-03	9.7644	1.01E-08
FAge*Fly	0.0066	5.69E-04	11.6570	1.33E-09
Ramp5	18.2485	5.3058	3.4393	9.93E-04
Ramp10	–4.8903	4.6801	–1.0449	0.2969
FAge20^2	–0.0072	0.0101	–0.7082	0.5137

million cargo aircraft fleets. Forecasts for both aircraft fleets were cut off at age 80, because that age is almost twice the range of previous Air Force experience.

As one might expect, Figure 5.1 shows that cargo aircraft fleets require more on-equipment work per flying hour throughout their service life than do fighters. The figure also shows the combined, but counteracting, effects of the two early-life ramp variables identified in the reduced equation in the historical data, one lasting five years, the other lasting ten. The shorter ramp appears to be a downward-sloping infantile-failure or learning-effect period where initially high on-equipment workloads decline steadily over the first five years. The longer trend appears to be an upward-sloping honeymoon pe-

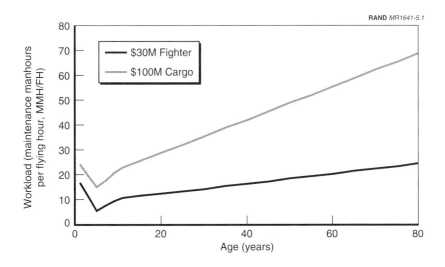

Figure 5.1—More-Expensive Aircraft On-Equipment Workloads Grow Faster

riod in which the workloads emerge steadily over the first ten years of fleet operation. After that time, the workload growth slows to a more moderate long-term rate.

We can see the effect of the positive Crgo variable in the initially higher on-equipment workloads. Typically, the larger aircraft requires more maintenance work to keep its systems serviceable, even in its early operations.

Those cargo aircraft workloads also grow faster because the aircraft is more expensive. The age–flyaway cost interaction term indicates that the $30-million fighter would find its workload would grow about

$$30 * .0067 = .20 \text{ MMH/FH}$$

per year it (after age 10 years), but the $100-million cargo aircraft would find that its workload would grow about

$$100 * .0067 = .67 \text{ MMH/FH}$$

per year. Of course, the regression equation indicates that a similarly priced fighter's workload would grow just as fast.

These growth rates are fairly modest, but not negligible. At a growth rate of .20 MMH/FH per year, a fighter flying 300 hours per year would require 60 additional maintenance manhours each year; a wing of 54 such aircraft would require 3,240 maintenance manhours, or about 1–2 additional maintenance personnel each year. For comparison, the $100-million cargo aircraft flying about 500 hours annually would require about 330 additional maintenance manhours each year; a cargo aircraft wing of 30 such aircraft would find its workload growing by over 10,000 hours, or 5–6 maintenance personnel each year.

At this point, a word of caution is warranted. The Air Force has never operated aircraft at the extreme ages past 40 years shown in Figure 5.1. Likewise, it has never operated a $100-million aircraft much past its second decade. Thus, we can expect the prediction errors to grow when considering aircraft fleets at ages much past 40 years or flyaway costs much higher than $100 million.

To provide some perspective on the possible error caused by extrapolating far beyond the available data, Figures 5.2 and 5.3 display the 95-percent confidence intervals for the fighter and cargo aircraft predictions using the regression equation from Table 5.2. The 95-percent confidence interval, the space between the heavy black and dashed black lines, is where we should expect that almost all fleets' on-equipment workloads would occur. Barely discernible, the two lines diverge very slightly as the fleet ages extend past age 40 toward age 80. That "fanning out" of the prediction error reflects the decreased reliability of forecasts made outside the range of the available data, assuming that the basic equation is correct.

Of course, it is possible that the equation may be wrong, especially if some new material-deterioration phenomena emerge as the fleets age. If those phenomena affect all fleets equally, the post–age-40 workload patterns would be expected to change; if they affect only some fleets, they would cause these error bands to expand more rapidly.

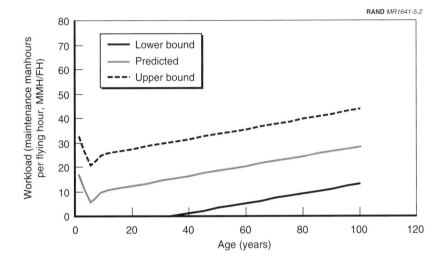

Figure 5.2—Fighters' On-Equipment Workloads Vary Widely for Reasons Other Than Age

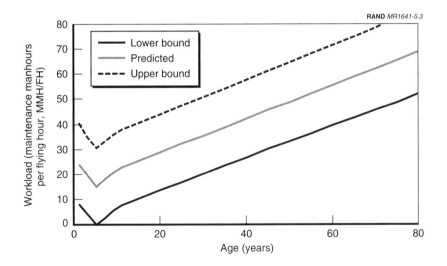

Figure 5.3—Cargo Aircraft On-Equipment Workloads Also Vary Widely, but the Age Effect Is More Apparent

In any case, both fleets' error bands are quite wide (about ±15 MMH/FH), indicating that individual fleet's workloads may vary considerably from the mean values depicted in Figure 5.1, either over time or across different fleets: Clearly, factors other than age and the other factors included in this analysis affect on-equipment (flightline) workloads. Those differences may be stable if they arise from idiosyncrasies in the design or manufacture of the MDS. They may also be unstable, if they arise from changes in usage or maintenance processes. We would need much longer historical data to distinguish how much of that variance is stable and how much is unstable. The majority of fleets' workloads will probably fall much closer than the bounds indicate; however, we should not be surprised if some fleets' on-equipment workloads sometimes diverged substantially from the predicted values, either over time or across fleets.

FINDINGS FOR OFF-EQUIPMENT WORKLOADS

The parameter coefficient estimates for the full compound regression of off-equipment workloads as aircraft fleets age are listed in Table 5.4. Once again, the significant variables in that table are those whose probabilities are less than 0.05. Remarkably, the significant variables in that table include many that were significant in the on-equipment equation. Although much of the off-equipment work is component diagnosis and repair at benches in a covered shop (as opposed to working on an uncovered aircraft outdoors), much of the off-equipment work is driven by removals and other on-equipment maintenance actions. Therefore, such similarities should not come as a surprise.

As with the full on-equipment workload regression, the cargo, tanker, trainer, and electronic command and control aircraft exhibited statistically significant differences in overall workload. The helo off-equipment workload (unavailable in the on-equipment data) was also significant. Also, as with the on-equipment analyses, the off-equipment regressions found a statistically significant effect for the interaction of flyaway cost and age.

Table 5.4

Age and Cost Affect Off-Equipment Workloads in the Full Regression

Results of regression analysis
Analysis Performed: Sun 03 Mar 2002 17:28:50
Data set used: D:\Documents\Dbases\Analysis\DataFiles\OffEq
Rule set used: D:\Documents\Dbases\Analysis\Rules\OffEq2

Dependent variable:	LWork
Total sum of squares	1.1195E+04
Regression sum of squares	3828.0919
Residual error	7366.4394
F-Statistic	11.3584
Degrees of freedom	21,459
R-squared	0.3420

Variable	Coefficient	Standard Error	t-Statistic	Probability
Constant	6.1292			
Bmbr	0.9198	1.2124	0.7587	0.5450
C2	−7.3689	1.0382	−7.0977	4.00E-07
Crgo	−4.0073	0.7205	−5.5619	6.59E-06
Helo	−4.0666	0.8185	−4.9685	2.32E-05
Tnkr	−6.4147	1.0638	−6.0302	2.63E-06
Trnr	−3.5528	1.1171	−3.1803	1.98E-03
AETC	0.1289	0.6657	0.1936	0.8409
AFE	0.6819	0.7703	0.8853	0.6198
AFR	0.6344	0.6652	0.9538	0.6574
AMC	−1.0120	0.9191	−1.1011	0.2707
ANG	1.1762	0.5816	2.0222	0.0411
PAF	1.4242	0.6530	2.1809	0.0278
SOC	5.4655	1.4442	3.7845	4.00E-04
Flyaway	−2.48E-03	3.02E-03	−0.8207	0.5825
Year98	0.2256	0.1355	1.6651	0.0925
FAge	8.91E-04	0.0468	0.0190	0.9824
FAge*Fly	2.22E-03	2.85E-04	7.7648	1.41E-07
Pulse5	−0.5797	1.4822	−0.3911	0.6982
Pulse10	0.9232	0.9460	0.9759	0.6691
Ramp5	−3.5259	4.5583	−0.7735	0.5541
Ramp10	0.4779	2.6592	0.1797	0.8517

However, this regression found a different workload pattern across MAJCOMs. While the on-equipment workloads in AFRC, AMC, and ANG differed significantly from those of the other commands in reporting on-equipment workloads, no such difference emerged in off-equipment workloads. Instead, Air National Guard, Pacific Air Forces, and Air Force Special Operations Command (SOC) off-equipment workloads differed significantly from those of other commands.

Also, the full off-equipment regression found no statistically significant effect related to aircraft flyaway cost. That finding stands in marked contrast to the fairly large effect (.041 MMH/FH per million dollars) found for on-equipment workloads. This suggests that the cross-platform differences in off-equipment workload are related to differences in primary mission, whereas flyaway-cost–related factors such as system complexity and weight have little, if any, influence on initial off-equipment workloads. (As noted above, flyaway cost does affect workload growth rates.)

Finally, none of the break-in variables was significant. Those variables are highly correlated, so it was still possible for one or more to emerge as the stepwise reduction was performed. The results of the stepwise backward regression are shown in Table 5.5.

We can see that all the variables that were statistically significant in the initial full regression remained significant in the reduced equation.

No Deceleration Was Detected in Off-Equipment Workloads

As shown in Table 5.6, $Age20^2$ was not significant at the .05 level when added to the reduced equation, so the regression found no evidence that off-equipment workloads accelerate or decelerate in late life. Therefore, we examined more closely the linear equation whose parameters are shown in Table 5.5.

Table 5.5

Age and Cost Affect Off-Equipment Workloads in the
Reduced Regression

Results of regression analysis
Analysis Performed: Sun 03 Mar 2002 17:37:26
Data set used: D:\Documents\Dbases\Analysis\DataFiles\OffEq
Rule set used: D:\Documents\Dbases\Analysis\Rules\OffEq2

Dependent variable:	LWork
Total sum of squares	1.1195E+04
Regression sum of squares	3593.5578
Residual error	7600.9735
F-Statistic	24.7419
Degrees of freedom	9,471
R-squared	0.3210

Variable	Coefficient	Standard Error	t-Statistic	Probability
Constant	6.2512			
C2	−7.7849	0.9588	−8.1192	8.34E-08
Crgo	−4.2060	0.5112	−8.2271	7.15E-08
Helo	−3.7614	0.7456	−5.0447	1.96E-05
Tnkr	−6.6942	0.6169	−10.8510	2.91E-09
Trnr	−4.0548	0.8491	−4.7755	3.57E-05
ANG	1.0936	0.4830	2.2640	0.0226
PAF	1.3537	0.5857	2.3114	0.0200
SOC	4.9170	1.3432	3.6606	5.51E-04
FAge*Fly	2.01E-03	1.99E-04	10.1212	6.47E-09

First, we examined Cook's distance and leverage values in a scatter-plot, and we found that all data points were within acceptable levels for Cook's distance. Thus, we found no evidence that any small subset of data points had undue influence on the results.

Practical Implications of the Off-Equipment Regression Equation

Figure 5.4 displays the forecasts of computed per-flying-hour expected-value off-equipment workloads for the $30-million fighter and the $100-million cargo aircraft fleets. The first thing we notice about these off-equipment workloads is that the more-expensive cargo aircraft starts with a lower workload than the fighter, but

Table 5.6

Off-Equipment Workloads Do Not Decelerate

Results of regression analysis
Analysis Performed: Sun 03 Mar 2002 17:38:57
Data set used: D:\Documents\Dbases\Analysis\DataFiles\OffEq
Rule set used: D:\Documents\Dbases\Analysis\Rules\OffEq2

Dependent variable:	LWork
Total sum of squares	1.1195E+04
Regression sum of squares	3596.8741
Residual error	7597.6573
F-Statistic	22.2507
Degrees of freedom	10,470
R-squared	0.3213

Variable	Coefficient	Standard Error	t-Statistic	Probability
Constant	6.4034			
C2	−7.8573	0.9729	−8.0765	8.87E-08
Crgo	−4.2164	0.5122	−8.2322	7.10E-08
Helo	−3.7372	0.7482	−4.9951	2.18E-05
Tnkr	−6.5410	0.7040	−9.2908	1.74E-08
Trnr	−4.0730	0.8507	−4.7876	3.48E-05
ANG	1.0726	0.4857	2.2085	0.0260
PAF	1.3610	0.5864	2.3209	0.0195
SOC	4.8620	1.3498	3.6019	6.43E-04
FAge*Fly	1.99E-03	2.02E-04	9.8591	8.77E-09
FAge20^2	−1.21E-03	2.67E-03	−0.4529	0.6556

catches up and passes the fighter off-equipment workload at about age 30. Not shown in the figure, the regression coefficients also indicate that the tankers, trainers, electronic command and control, and helicopter aircraft will also start their service lives with smaller off-equipment workloads than fighters. The relatively more-complex and state-of-the-art fighters, bombers, and U-2 aircraft, with their more expensive and delicate onboard avionics equipment, generate substantially higher initial workloads than the other aircraft. (In passing, note that the electronic command and control aircraft does have highly sophisticated electronic suites, but much of their off-equipment maintenance work is performed by contractor logistics support personnel. Those workloads are analyzed later in this chapter.)

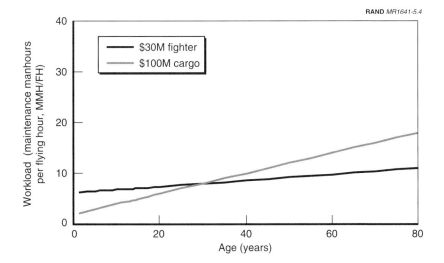

Figure 5.4—Off-Equipment Workloads for the More-Expensive Cargo
Aircraft Overtake Fighter Workloads at About Age 30

As with the on-equipment findings, the reduced equation indicates
that off-equipment workloads grow with age, and that the workloads
of the more-expensive platforms grow more rapidly. That growth is
rapid enough to catch up with the fighter workload per flying hour by
about age 30, despite a much larger initial workload for the fighter.
Thus, the $30-million fighter off-equipment workload grows about
.06 MMH/FH annually, and the $100-million cargo aircraft workload
grows about .20 MMH/FH. A wing of 54 fighters flying 300 hours per
aircraft per year would generate only about 972 additional maintenance manhours annually (about one additional person every two
years). A wing of 30 cargo aircraft flying 500 hours per year would
generate about 3,000 additional maintenance hours (between one
and two additional personnel per year).

Once again, these forecasts should be viewed with some caution, because the Air Force has little experience operating fleets for such extended periods. Figures 5.5 and 5.6 display the 95-percent confidence bounds for the fighter and cargo aircraft, respectively. The
"fan-out" at higher ages is practically invisible, although a very small
effect is present.

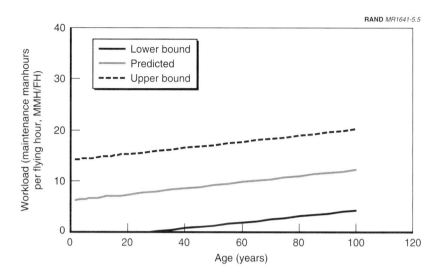

Figure 5.5—Fighters' Off-Equipment Workloads Vary Widely for Reasons
Other Than Age

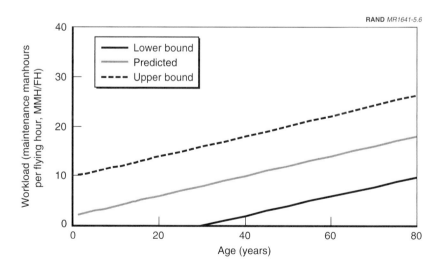

Figure 5.6—Cargo Aircraft Off-Equipment Workloads Vary Widely for
Reasons Other Than Age

Of course, we can also see the relatively large range of possible workload variations for these fleets at any age. The fleets' workloads should wander outside those boundaries only rarely, but we should not be surprised to observe individual fleets' workloads anywhere within these boundaries. Clearly, many factors other than age and those included in these equations affect off-equipment workloads.

FINDINGS FOR BASE PERIODIC-INSPECTION WORKLOADS

Table 5.7 shows the parameter coefficient estimates for the full regression of base periodic-inspection workloads as aircraft fleets age. In contrast to the on- and off-equipment regressions, no continuous age-related variables were statistically significant in the full base periodic-inspection regression. Trainers', bombers', and C-130s' periodic-inspection workloads were significantly different (the first lower and the latter two higher) than fighters'. Similarly, the regression identified AMC and ANG as having lower and higher base periodic-inspection workloads, respectively. It also found the flyaway cost and the two 5-year break-in variables significant. Finally, the regression found a statistically significant relationship between flyaway cost and base periodic-inspection workload.

A Stepwise Backward Regression Reduced the Independent Variables

Again, we used a stepwise backward regression to eliminate the nonsignificant regression variables progressively. Variables were removed one at a time until all coefficients had probabilities of .05 or less.

In Table 5.8, which displays the final results from that process, we can see that all the variables that were statistically significant in the initial full regression remained significant in the reduced equation.

Table 5.7

Age Does Not Affect Base Periodic-Inspection Workloads
in the Full Regression

Results of regression analysis
Analysis Performed: Sun 03 Mar 2002 19:47:02
Data set used:
D:\Documents\Dbases\Analysis\DataFiles\PhaseSpec
Rule set used:
D:\Documents\Dbases\Analysis\Rules\PhaseRules

Dependent variable:	LPhs			
Total sum of squares	259.1517			
Regression sum of squares	154.5981			
Residual error	104.5536			
F-Statistic	8.9423			
Degrees of freedom	21,127			
R-squared	0.5966			
Variable	Coefficient	Standard Error	t-Statistic	Probability
Constant	0.7604			
C2	0.3125	0.5110	0.6117	0.5490
C130	0.6682	0.3188	2.0963	0.0357
U2	0.7993	0.4979	1.6053	0.1069
Trnr	−1.4204	0.4981	−2.8513	0.0053
Bmbr	1.7781	0.8934	1.9901	0.0459
Tnkr	−0.0243	0.4608	−0.0527	0.9570
AET	0.2443	0.3210	0.7611	0.5455
AFE	−0.3965	0.2883	−1.3755	0.1679
AFR	−0.1015	0.3067	−0.3308	0.7406
AMC	−0.9945	0.4071	−2.4427	0.0152
ANG	1.1253	0.2369	4.7501	5.03E-05
PAF	−0.4419	0.2553	−1.7310	0.0820
SOC	−0.8977	0.7037	−1.2757	0.2016
FAge	0.0250	0.0202	1.2362	0.2162
Flyaway	0.0097	3.11E-03	3.1267	2.57E-03
Year98	−0.2261	0.1528	−1.4800	0.1374
FAge*Fly	−2.90E-04	2.20E-04	−1.3160	0.1874
Pulse5	−12.7387	3.5538	−3.5845	7.92E-04
Pulse10	0.3142	0.3553	0.8844	0.6181
Ramp5	15.5699	4.3453	3.5832	7.94E-04
Ramp10	−0.8104	1.0676	−0.7591	0.5443

Table 5.8

**Age Does Not Affect Base Periodic Inspections in the
Reduced Regression**

Results of regression analysis
Analysis Performed: Sun 03 Mar 2002 19:54:02
Data set used:
D:\Documents\Dbases\Analysis\DataFiles\PhaseSpec
Rule set used: D:\Documents\Dbases\Analysis\Rules\PhaseRules

Dependent variable:	LPhs			
Total sum of squares	259.1517			
Regression sum of squares	141.5186			
Residual error	117.6331			
F-Statistic	21.0534			
Degrees of freedom	8,140			
R-squared	0.5461			

Variable	Coefficient	Standard Error	t-Statistic	Probability
Constant	1.0715			
Bmbr	1.4440	0.6994	2.0646	0.0383
C130	0.8387	0.2124	3.9494	3.12E-04
Trnr	−0.6778	0.3284	−2.0639	0.0384
AMC	−0.7671	0.3681	−2.0841	0.0366
ANG	1.2910	0.1972	6.5476	1.54E-06
Flyaway	0.0080	1.88E-03	4.2437	1.54E-04
Pulse5	−11.7397	2.4627	−4.7670	4.68E-05
Ramp5	14.4626	3.1724	4.5589	7.43E-05

No Deceleration Was Detected in Base Periodic-Inspection Workloads

In Table 5.9, the Age20^2 factor is not significant at the .05 level when added to the reduced equation, which indicates that the regression found no evidence that base periodic-inspection workloads accelerate or decelerate in late life. Therefore, we examined more closely the linear equation whose parameters are shown in Table 5.9.

First, we examined Cook's distance and leverage values in a scatterplot. In this regression, two data points were not within acceptable levels for Cook's distance, and they were the two points with the greatest leverage: values for B-2A periodic inspections in ACC, which

Table 5.9

Base Periodic-Inspection Workloads Do Not Accelerate
or Decelerate

Results of regression analysis
Analysis Performed: Sun 03 Mar 2002 19:55:51
Data set used:
D:\Documents\Dbases\Analysis\DataFiles\PhaseSpec
Rule set used: D:\Documents\Dbases\Analysis\Rules\PhaseRules

Dependent variable:	LPhs			
Total sum of squares	259.1517			
Regression sum of squares	141.5208			
Residual error	117.6309			
F-Statistic	18.5811			
Degrees of freedom	9,139			
R-squared	0.5461			

Variable	Coefficient	Standard Error	t-Statistic	Probability
Constant	1.0770			
Bmbr	1.4464	0.7034	2.0562	0.0391
C130	0.8386	0.2131	3.9347	3.24E-04
Trnr	−0.6771	0.3299	−2.0527	0.0394
AMC	−0.7644	0.3733	−2.0478	0.0399
ANG	1.2909	0.1979	6.5234	1.61E-06
Flyaway	0.0080	1.90E-03	4.1878	1.76E-04
Pulse5	−11.7195	2.5030	−4.6822	5.65E-05
Ramp5	14.4529	3.1895	4.5314	7.92E-05
$Age20^2$	−4.36E-05	8.56E-04	−0.0510	0.9583

were substantially different from other nearby values. A regression analysis that eliminated those values did not find the two 5-year break-in variables significant. The main effect of the B-2 data points was to support an infantile-failure hypothesis, because B-2A periodic-inspection workloads dropped dramatically between 1997 and 1998 while that fleet increased from 3.6 to 4.6 years of age. Thus, eliminating those data caused a small overall increase in the constant (from 1.07 to 1.24) and a larger increase in the bomber categorical variable (from 1.44 to 2.48). Thus, the equation without the B2 data implies that all aircraft have slightly higher base periodic inspection workloads and that there is no break-in period. In addition, the analysis without those data suggests that the difference between bombers and fighters might be larger.

Although eliminating the two data points yielded a simpler equation, there is no evidence that those two points do not accurately reflect the actual workloads for those fleets. If so, those points provide additional information about the underlying workload pattern as fleets age. With time, additional historical experience will confirm whether the infantile break-in pattern in Table 5.8 exists.

Once past that period, the two equations give strikingly similar forecasts for all but the bomber fleets. Both suggest a steady-state period after the first five years of operation, with only a few differences across fleets and commands (i.e., bombers, trainers, C-130s, ANG, and AMC), once differences in flyaway cost are accounted for.

Practical Implications of the Periodic-Inspection-Workload Regression Equation

Figure 5.7 displays the computed per-flying-hour expected-value periodic-inspection workload forecasts for the $30-million fighter and the $100-million cargo aircraft fleets. The cargo aircraft workload calculations in that figure assumed that this cargo aircraft would experience the same periodic-inspection offset as the C-130.

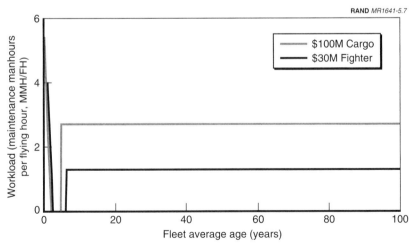

Figure 5.7—Base Periodic-Inspection Workloads Do Not Increase as Fleets Age

The forecast shows no long-term age-related growth for either aircraft. However, the reduced equation (retaining the B-2A data points) depicts a highly unstable period during the very early fleet operational period. According to the reduced regression equation, we might expect an initial flurry of periodic-inspection work in the first one to three years of a fleet's life. After the first five years, the workload would assume a stable level ever after.

As with the on- and off-equipment workloads, we can see a distinct difference between the cargo aircraft steady-state workload (2.7 MMH/FH) and the fighter aircraft workload (1.3 MMH/FH). That difference arises from the combined effects of the C-130 categorical variable (0.8 MMH/FH) and the differences in flyaway costs (0.6 MMH/FH).

Even though no age-related growth is projected in the reduced regression equation, a prediction error is still present, as shown in Figures 5.8 and 5.9. In contrast to the on-equipment and off-equipment equations, no error "fan out" occurs as the fleet ages, because the regression found no significant effect for age. As with the on-equipment (flightline) workloads and off-equipment workloads, those higherror bounds reflect the influence of factors other than flyaway cost, using command, and basic mission.

FINDINGS FOR SPECIAL-INSPECTION WORKLOADS

The parameter coefficient estimates for the full regression of special-inspection workloads as aircraft fleets age are presented in Table 5.10. The full regression found a relationship between age and late-life special-inspection workloads. In contrast to the on- and off-equipment regressions, the full special-inspection regression found only a simple growth rate (.0235 MMH/FH per year), not one that varied depending on the aircraft flyaway cost. C-130s, trainers, tankers, U-2s, and electronic command and control aircraft had special-inspection workload levels significantly lower than those of fighters. The regression also identified the ANG and AFRC as having significantly higher special-inspection workloads; USAFE had a lower one. It also found the flyaway cost, the two 5-year break-in variables, and the 10-year pulse break-in variable significant.

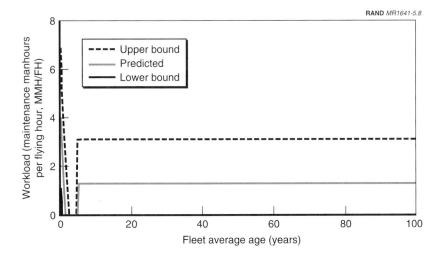

Figure 5.8—Fighters' Periodic Inspections Vary Widely

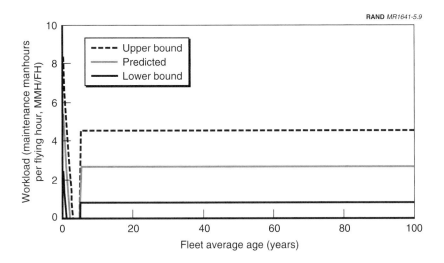

**Figure 5.9—Cargo Aircraft Periodic Inspections Also Vary Widely,
but Around a Higher Mean**

Table 5.10

Age Affects Special Inspections in the Full Regression

Results of regression analysis
Analysis Performed: Sun 03 Mar 2002 20:09:44
Data set used:
D:\Documents\Dbases\Analysis\DataFiles\PhaseSpec
Rule set used:
D:\Documents\Dbases\Analysis\Rules\PhaseRules

Dependent variable:	LSpec			
Total sum of squares	187.5422			
Regression sum of squares	154.0700			
Residual error	33.4722			
F-Statistic	27.8367			
Degrees of freedom	21,127			
R-squared	0.8215			
Variable	Coefficient	Standard Error	t-Statistic	Probability
Constant	1.3198			
Bmbr	−0.5279	0.5055	−1.0443	0.2987
C2	−2.5313	0.2891	−8.7553	7.11E-08
C130	−1.5523	0.1804	−8.6067	8.54E-08
Tnkr	−2.0230	0.2608	−7.7582	2.60E-07
Trnr	−1.6412	0.2819	−5.8226	5.81E-06
U2	−0.7702	0.2817	−2.7338	0.0072
AETC	0.0323	0.1816	0.1780	0.8532
AFE	−0.3558	0.1631	−2.1813	0.0291
AFR	0.3439	0.1736	1.9816	0.0468
AMC	−0.2645	0.2304	−1.1484	0.2516
ANG	0.6433	0.1340	4.7991	4.52E-05
PAF	−0.0973	0.1444	−0.6737	0.5088
SOC	0.0757	0.3982	0.1902	0.8437
FAge	0.0235	0.0114	2.0542	0.0395
Flyaway	0.0069	1.76E-03	3.9300	3.35E-04
Year98	0.0843	0.0865	0.9747	0.6671
FAge*Fly	1.01E-04	1.25E-04	0.8126	0.5766
Pulse5	−5.6911	2.0108	−2.8303	0.0056
Pulse10	0.4178	0.2010	2.0786	0.0373
Ramp5	8.2540	2.4586	3.3572	1.42E-03
Ramp10	−0.5686	0.6040	−0.9413	0.6494

A Stepwise Backward Regression Reduced the Independent Variables

Again, we used a stepwise backward regression to eliminate the nonsignificant regression variables progressively, one at a time, until all coefficients had probabilities of .05 or less. Table 5.11 displays the final results from that process.

In the table, we can see that all the variables that were statistically significant in the initial full regression remained significant in the reduced equation. No previously nonsignificant variables emerged as significant in the reduced equation.

No Deceleration Was Detected in Special Inspections

In Table 5.12, the FAge20^2 factor is not significant at the .05 level when added to the reduced equations; therefore, the regression provides no evidence that special-inspection workloads accelerate or decelerate in late life.

We examined more closely the linear equation whose parameters are shown in Table 5.11.

First, we examined Cook's distance and leverage values in a scatterplot. All data points were within acceptable levels for Cook's distance. Thus, there is no evidence that a small subset of data points had undue influence on the results.

Table 5.11

Age Affects Special Inspections in the Reduced Regression

Results of regression analysis
Analysis Performed: Sun 03 Mar 2002 20:15:28
Data set used:
D:\Documents\Dbases\Analysis\DataFiles\PhaseSpec
Rule set used: D:\Documents\Dbases\Analysis\Rules\PhaseRules

Dependent variable:	LSpec			
Total sum of squares	187.5422			
Regression sum of squares	152.6581			
Residual error	34.8842			
F-Statistic	45.4445			
Degrees of freedom	13,135			
R-squared	0.8140			

Variable	Coefficient	Standard Error	t-Statistic	Probability
Constant	1.1353			
C2	−2.2695	0.1914	−11.8546	2.82E-09
C130	−1.6385	0.1584	−10.3458	1.15E-08
U2	−0.6694	0.2685	−2.4930	0.0133
Tnkr	−2.1067	0.2443	−8.6216	7.93E-08
Trnr	−1.7437	0.2454	−7.1042	6.46E-07
AFE	−0.3278	0.1472	−2.2277	0.0259
AFR	0.4113	0.1545	2.6620	0.0086
ANG	0.6816	0.1146	5.9464	4.48E-06
FAge	0.0321	0.0098	3.2957	1.64E-03
Flyaway	0.0066	7.46E-04	8.8859	5.74E-08
Pulse5	−5.3755	1.3278	−4.0484	2.47E-04
Pulse10	0.3638	0.1478	2.4609	0.0144
Ramp5	7.1546	1.8505	3.8663	3.86E-04

Table 5.12

Special-Inspection Workloads Do Not Decelerate

Results of regression analysis
Analysis Performed: Sun 03 Mar 2002 20:18:54
Data set used:
D:\Documents\Dbases\Analysis\DataFiles\PhaseSpec
Rule set used: D:\Documents\Dbases\Analysis\Rules\PhaseRules

Dependent variable:	LSpec			
Total sum of squares	187.5422			
Regression sum of squares	152.8871			
Residual error	34.6551			
F-Statistic	42.2260			
Degrees of freedom	14,134			
R-squared	0.8152			

Variable	Coefficient	Standard Error	t-Statistic	Probability
Constant	1.1440			
C2	−2.3284	0.2015	−11.5555	3.69E-09
C130	−1.6101	0.1613	−9.9828	1.68E-08
Tnkr	−1.9211	0.3141	−6.1163	3.31E-06
Trnr	−1.6982	0.2502	−6.7864	1.07E-06
U2	−0.7046	0.2712	−2.5980	0.0101
AFE	−0.3337	0.1474	−2.2641	0.0237
AFR	0.4197	0.1548	2.7104	0.0076
ANG	0.6712	0.1152	5.8261	5.61E-06
FAge	0.0352	0.0103	3.4235	1.18E-03
Flyaway	0.0067	7.52E-04	8.9307	5.48E-08
Pulse5	−5.4507	1.3308	−4.0959	2.21E-04
Pulse10	0.4896	0.1994	2.4558	0.0146
Ramp5	7.6245	1.9174	3.9764	2.95E-04
FAge20^2	−1.07E-03	1.14E-03	−0.9411	0.6494

Practical Implications of the Reduced Equations

Figure 5.10 displays the computed forecasts for special-inspection workloads for the $30-million fighter and the $100-million cargo aircraft fleets. The cargo aircraft workload in that figure assumed that most cargo aircraft would experience the same special-inspection offset as the C-130.

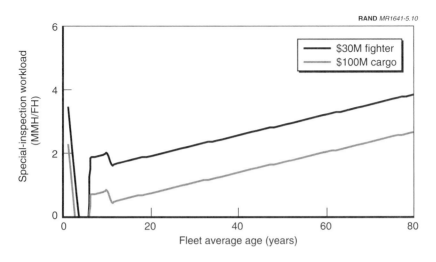

Figure 5.10—Special Inspections for Fighter and Cargo Aircraft Grow at Equal Rates

Although they start at different levels, the workloads for both aircraft grow at the same rate as the two fleets age, so the later-life workloads follow parallel tracks. Also, it would appear that the early-life workloads are even more unstable than the periodic-inspection workloads: An initial high peak is followed by a lull (as for the periodic inspections), but a small surge occurs in the second five years of operation. After the first ten years, the workload appears to settle down into a modest growth rate.

The C-130 variable, which had a positive effect in the periodic-inspection regression, now has a large negative effect on special-inspection workloads. In fact, it substantially outweighs the effect of the flyaway-cost variable on the cargo aircraft special-inspection workload. Specifically, the $100-million flyaway cost contributes only 0.7 MMH/FH, whereas the C-130 categorical variable is a more noticeable –1.6 MMH/FH. Indeed, all the other platforms except bombers have lower special-inspection workloads than fighters. Even though the bombers have a small negative coefficient in Table 5.10, the backward regression analysis found that that coefficient is not significant. Thus, bombers' higher workloads are fully explained by their higher flyaway cost.

As Figure 5.11 shows for a fighter aircraft and Figure 5.12 shows for a cargo aircraft (still using the C-130 categorical variable), the range of likely special-inspection workloads increases as the aircraft age increases. This is the first case for which that growth is easily perceived on the graph. It indicates that the regression equation's accuracy will deteriorate slightly after fleets pass age 40 years.

REPAIR-COST FINDINGS FOR DEPOT-LEVEL REPARABLE COMPONENTS

The parameter coefficient estimates for the full regression of depot-level reparable (DLR) repair costs as aircraft fleets age are listed in Table 5.13. The full regression found a significant positive relationship between DLR repair costs and the interaction between age and flyaway cost. It also found a negative relationship between those costs and flyaway cost, and that helicopters, electronic command and control aircraft, cargo aircraft, and tankers had overall DLR repair costs significantly lower than those of fighters. Only bombers had significantly higher DLR repair costs.

A Stepwise Backward Regression Reduced the Independent Variables

We used a stepwise backward regression to eliminate the nonsignificant regression variables progressively, one at a time, until all coefficients had probabilities of .05 or less. Table 5.14 displays the final results from that process.

We can see in the table that all the variables that were statistically significant in the initial full regression remained significant, and that none of the other variables became significant.

No Deceleration Was Found in DLR Repair Costs

As Table 5.15 shows, the second-order age term was not statistically significant at the .05 level in the regression. Therefore, we examined more closely the linear equation whose parameters are shown in Table 5.13.

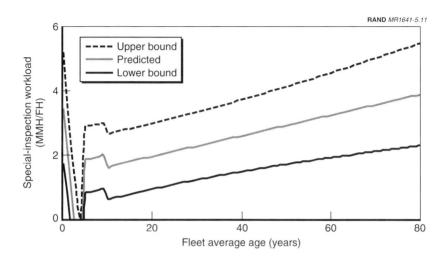

Figure 5.11—The Predicted Variability of Fighter Special-Inspection
Workloads Increases as Fleets Age

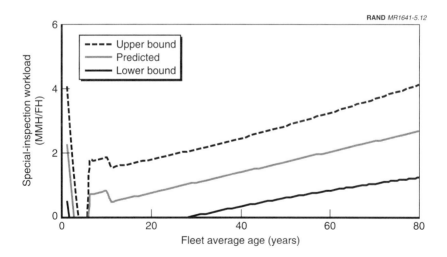

Figure 5.12—The Predicted Variability of Cargo Aircraft Special-Inspection
Workloads Also Grows as Fleets Age

First, we examined Cook's distance and leverage values in a scatter-plot and found that all data points were within acceptable levels for Cook's distance.

Table 5.13

Age Affects Depot-Level-Reparable Repair Costs in the Full Regression

Results of regression analysis
Analysis Performed: Sun 03 Mar 2002 22:03:06
Data set used:
D:\Documents\Dbases\Analysis\DataFiles\DeflDLRCost
Rule set used:
D:\Documents\Dbases\Analysis\Rules\ConsDLRCostRules

Dependent variable:	LRep$	
Total sum of squares	1.5684E+09	
Regression sum of squares	8.2014E+08	
Residual error	7.4822E+08	
F-Statistic	12.7620	
Degrees of freedom	14,163	
R-squared	0.5229	

Variable	Coefficient	Standard Error	t-Statistic	Probability
Constant	3794.6832			
Bmbr	3306.3425	911.6771	3.6267	6.77E-04
C2	−3120.1353	786.0159	−3.9696	2.87E-04
Crgo	−3045.4298	569.5272	−5.3473	1.31E-05
Helo	−3811.4791	707.3309	−5.3885	1.20E-05
Tnkr	−3921.2872	971.2723	−4.0373	2.43E-04
Trnr	−819.4107	734.4513	−1.1157	0.2653
FAge	26.1081	36.7539	0.7104	0.5144
Flyaway	−7.3895	1.4049	−5.2600	1.56E-05
Year98	−90.2363	86.4848	−1.0434	0.2987
FAge*Fly	0.7562	0.2235	3.3834	1.27E-03
Pulse5	−1554.6611	1235.8602	−1.2580	0.2075
Pulse10	1530.8101	1022.9941	1.4964	0.1325
Ramp5	3934.5139	2167.3392	1.8154	0.0677
Ramp10	−2841.4923	3019.0677	−0.9412	0.6498

Practical Implications of the Regression Equation for DLR Repair Requirements

In Figure 5.13, which displays the forecast computed per-flying-hour expected-value DLR repair requirements for the $30-million fighter and the $100-million cargo aircraft fleets, we can see that the fighter would require more DLR repair expenditures per flying hour throughout its first 60 years of operation than would the cargo aircraft. (Fighters are only rarely operated beyond 30 years.) Both the negative cargo coefficient and the negative flyaway-cost coefficient contribute to that effect. The $100-million flyaway cost lowers the basic requirement by $790 per flying hour, and the cargo coefficient lowers it another $2,940 (see Table 5.14).

Table 5.14

Age Affects Depot-Level-Reparable Repair Costs in the Reduced Regression

Results of regression analysis
Analysis Performed: Sun 03 Mar 2002 22:07:15
Data set used:
D:\Documents\Dbases\Analysis\DataFiles\DeflDLRCost
Rule set used:
D:\Documents\Dbases\Analysis\Rules\ConsDLRCostRules

Dependent variable:	LRep$
Total sum of squares	1.5684E+09
Regression sum of squares	7.8437E+08
Residual error	7.8399E+08
F-Statistic	24.2975
Degrees of freedom	7,170
R-squared	0.5001

Variable	Coefficient	Standard Error	t-Statistic	Probability
Constant	4210.6569			
Bmbr	4179.4321	771.9352	5.4142	1.12E-05
C2	−2487.8963	736.5361	−3.3778	1.28E-03
Cargo	−2489.9831	471.1592	−5.2848	1.46E-05
Helo	−3426.2010	632.1326	−5.4201	1.11E-05
Tnkr	−3098.7809	669.2529	−4.6302	5.97E-05
Flyaway	−7.9061	0.9541	−8.2865	1.02E-07
FAge*Fly	0.6626	0.1875	3.5347	8.51E-04

Table 5.15

Depot-Level-Reparable Repair Costs Did Not Decelerate
with Age

Results of regression analysis
Analysis Performed: Sun 03 Mar 2002 22:08:55
Data set used:
D:\Documents\Dbases\Analysis\DataFiles\DeflDLRCost
Rule set used:
D:\Documents\Dbases\Analysis\Rules\ConsDLRCostRules

Dependent variable:	LRep$
Total sum of squares	1.5684E+09
Regression sum of squares	7.8453E+08
Residual error	7.8383E+08
F-Statistic	21.1438
Degrees of freedom	8,169
R-squared	0.5002

Variable	Coefficient	Standard Error	t-Statistic	Probability
Constant	4173.9865			
Bmbr	4139.6890	803.5187	5.1520	1.93E-05
C2	−2491.9173	738.9586	−3.3722	1.30E-03
Cargo	−2509.1390	483.7646	−5.1867	1.79E-05
Helo	−3433.7444	635.2518	−5.4053	1.15E-05
Tnkr	−3165.2077	761.5448	−4.1563	1.81E-04
Flyaway	−7.9873	1.0531	−7.5847	2.73E-07
FAge*Fly	0.6781	0.2059	3.2937	1.59E-03
FAge20^2	0.3785	2.0503	0.1846	0.8480

Nevertheless, the more-expensive cargo aircraft's requirement grows more rapidly, because of the age–flyaway cost interaction term. Thus, the fighter's DLR requirement would grow about $20 per flying hour each year, but the cargo aircraft's requirement would grow over three times as fast, at $66 per flying hour per year. In that case, the fighter flying 300 hours per year would encounter DLR repair cost growth of about $6,000 additional repair demands per year, and the cargo aircraft flying 500 hours per year would experience annual growth of about $33,000. Each fighter of a wing of 54 fighters flying 300 hours per year would cause the USAF's DLR repair costs to grow about $320,000 annually, whereas each cargo aircraft wing of 30 flying 500 hours per year would cause about $990,000 annual growth.

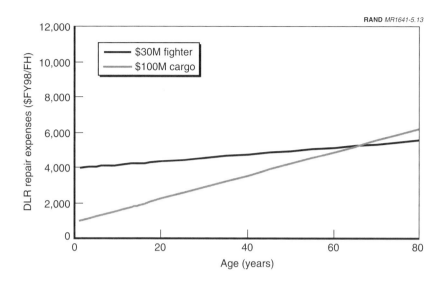

Figure 5.13—DLR Repair Expenditures Grow Steadily as Aircraft Age

Despite the difference in their annual growth rates, it would take over 60 years for the cargo aircraft's DLR repair costs per flying hour to catch up with the fighter's.

While it is difficult to see in Figure 5.14, which shows how aircraft age affects the range of likely DLR repair requirements for a fighter aircraft, the range of likely DLR repair requirements fans out as the aircraft age increases. The fanning-out is more noticeable in Figure 5.15, which shows DLR repair requirements for the more-expensive cargo aircraft.

FINDINGS FOR GENERAL STOCK DIVISION MATERIAL CONSUMPTION

Table 5.16 shows the parameter coefficient estimates for the full regression of General Stock Division (GSD) material expenditures as aircraft fleets age. The full regression found the age–flyaway cost interaction term (FAge*Fly) significantly related to GSD consumption,

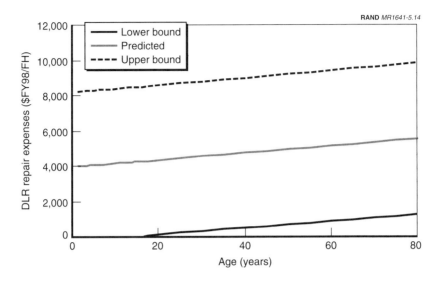

Figure 5.14—DLR Repair Expenditures for Fighters Vary Widely

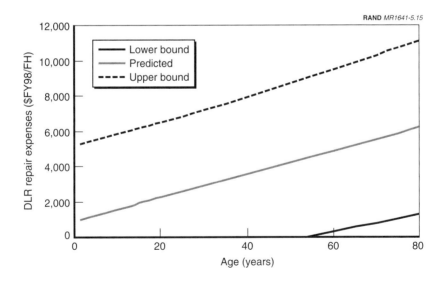

**Figure 5.15—Variability in DLR Repair Expenditures for Cargo Aircraft
Increases Noticeably as Fleets Age**

Table 5.16

Age Affects GSD Material Consumption in the Full Regression

Results of regression analysis
Analysis Performed: Sun 03 Nov 2002 13:19:49
Data set used: D:\Documents\Dbases\Analysis\DataFiles\GSD98
Rule set used: D:\Documents\Dbases\Analysis\Rules\GSDRules

Dependent variable:	LGSD			
Total sum of squares	1.2109E+07			
Regression sum of squares	7.0091E+06			
Residual error	5.1000E+06			
F-Statistic	10.4451			
Degrees of freedom	15,114			
R-squared	0.5788			

Variable	Coefficient	Standard Error	t-Statistic	Probability
Constant	287.4290			
Bmbr	192.8987	129.3419	1.4914	0.1347
C2	−95.1203	71.6854	−1.3269	0.1840
Crgo	87.2995	56.5587	1.5435	0.1215
Helo	238.8953	82.3578	2.9007	4.71E-03
OSA	−295.0503	130.4030	−2.2626	0.0240
Tnkr	−195.6274	95.5192	−2.0480	0.0403
Trnr	−166.4232	85.8521	−1.9385	0.0520
FAge	−2.5112	2.4254	−1.0354	0.3032
Flyaway	0.8325	0.3260	2.5535	0.0116
Year98	20.9553	19.0593	1.0995	0.2733
FAge*Fly	0.0615	0.0286	2.1499	0.0316
Pulse5	45.1378	307.5338	0.1468	0.8783
Pulse10	133.7486	142.2513	0.9402	0.6486
Ramp5	808.1896	603.2654	1.3397	0.1797
Ramp10	−1085.1191	780.9641	−1.3895	0.1638

in addition to its direct relationship to flyaway cost. Helicopters generally consume more GSD material than other aircraft (after controlling for flyaway cost and age), whereas the operational support aircraft (OSA) and tanker (Tnkr) fleets consume less, according to the full regression equation.

A Stepwise Backward Regression Reduced the Independent Variables

We used a stepwise backward regression to eliminate the nonsignificant regression variables progressively, one at a time, until all coefficients had probabilities of .05 or less. Table 5.17 displays the final results of that process.

We can see that all the variables that were significant in the full regression remained significant in the reduced equation. In addition, the trainer (Trnr) and electronic command and control (C2) aircraft emerged as significant in the reduced equation.

Table 5.17

Age Affects GSD Material Consumption in the Reduced Regression

Results of regression analysis
Analysis Performed: Sun 03 Nov 2002 13:24:05
Data set used: D:\Documents\Dbases\Analysis\DataFiles\GSD98
Rule set used: D:\Documents\Dbases\Analysis\Rules\GSDRules

Dependent variable:	LGSD			
Total sum of squares	1.2109E+07			
Regression sum of squares	6.6373E+06			
Residual error	5.4718E+06			
F-Statistic	21.1412			
Degrees of freedom	7,122			
R-squared	0.5481			

Variable	Coefficient	Standard Error	t-Statistic	Probability
Constant	312.3085			
C2	−194.0184	53.2284	−3.6450	6.86E-04
Helo	191.3058	75.6426	2.5291	0.0122
OSA	−339.7048	125.2311	−2.7126	0.0076
Tnkr	−299.1704	79.8740	−3.7455	5.34E-04
Trnr	−239.4651	72.8755	−3.2859	1.71E-03
Flyaway	0.6134	0.1786	3.4343	1.17E-03
FAge*Fly	0.0884	0.0217	4.0716	2.41E-04

Deceleration Was Statistically Significant in GSD Consumption

As shown in Table 5.18, the $FAge20^2$ factor detected a significant deceleration in GSD material consumption as aircraft fleets age. Presumably, the equation with the second-order term better predicts the likely GSD consumption, at least for the range of the data available for this study. Therefore, the second-order equation whose parameters are shown in Table 5.18 was examined more closely.

First, we examined Cook's distance and leverage values in a scatterplot and found that all data points were within acceptable levels for Cook's distance, even the points near the high end of the leverage scale. Thus, there is no evidence that a small subset of data points unduly influenced the results.

Table 5.18

Deceleration in the GSD Material Consumption Regression Was Significant

Results of regression analysis				
Analysis Performed: Sun 03 Nov 2002 13:25:31				
Data set used: D:\Documents\Dbases\Analysis\DataFiles\GSD98				
Rule set used: D:\Documents\Dbases\Analysis\Rules\GSDRules				
Dependent variable:	LGSD			
Total sum of squares	1.2109E+07			
Regression sum of squares	6.8243E+06			
Residual error	5.2848E+06			
F-Statistic	19.5311			
Degrees of freedom	8,121			
R-squared	0.5636			
Variable	Coefficient	Standard Error	t-Statistic	Probability
Constant	359.8281			
C2	−184.8920	52.7117	−3.5076	9.72E-04
Helo	172.4028	75.2026	2.2925	0.0222
OSA	−365.5762	124.2114	−2.9432	4.18E-03
Tnkr	−241.7727	83.5605	−2.8934	4.76E-03
Trnr	−213.9707	72.9629	−2.9326	4.30E-03
Flyaway	0.6485	0.1771	3.6625	6.58E-04
FAge*Fly	0.0846	0.0215	3.9354	3.35E-04
$FAge20^2$	−0.3221	0.1557	−2.0690	0.0382

Practical Implications of the Regression Equation for GSD Requirements

Figure 5.16 displays the computed per-flying-hour expected-value GSD material consumption forecasts for the $30-million fighter and the $100-million cargo aircraft fleets, assuming that the second-order deceleration occurs. From the figure, we can see that both aircraft fleets' GSD consumption initially grows slowly over the first 20 years, after which the fighter aircraft's GSD consumption levels out and (according to the forecast) begins to decline. The cargo fleet's GSD consumption levels out about age 30 and begins to decline after that, according to the regression equation.

This figure also shows one of the potential pitfalls of extrapolating trends far past USAF experience: Accepting these forecasts at face value might tempt budget planners to reduce GSD funds accordingly. Of course, the USAF has operated few fighter fleets much past age 20, and it has operated very few other fleets past age 40. Obviously, the second-order equation fits the historical experience better than the linear equation does, but it has probably over-interpreted the early-to-mid-life growth deceleration as a process that will continue into later life. Given the available data, we consider it equally

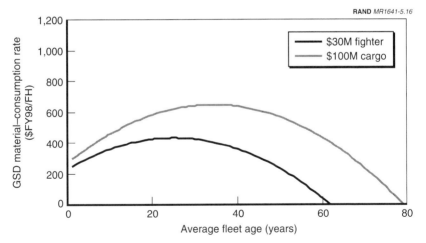

Figure 5.16—More-Expensive Cargo Aircraft Experience Greater Initial Growth in GSD Consumption

possible that the GSD consumption could simply stabilize at those mature levels. If so, these forecasts will need to be revised substantially as more historical data for older fleets become available.

The uncertainties associated with limited history become more visible when we consider the 95-percent confidence intervals on the forecasts, in Figure 5.17 for the $30-million fighter GSD consumption and in Figure 5.18 for the $100-million cargo aircraft. Even though predicted mean values diminish according to the basic forecast, the upper confidence-interval bounds in both figures begin to diverge shortly after the mean prediction reaches its peak. Thus, as aircraft age increases past the range of the current Air Force experience, the range of likely GSD consumption costs fans out more than do costs for most other categories in this study.

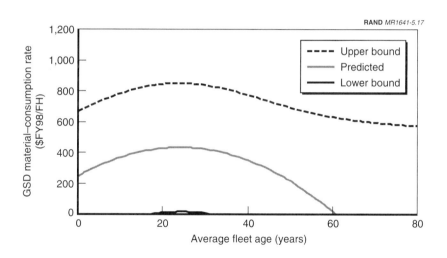

Figure 5.17—Fighters' GSD Consumption Becomes Less Predictable as Fleets Age Past Age 30

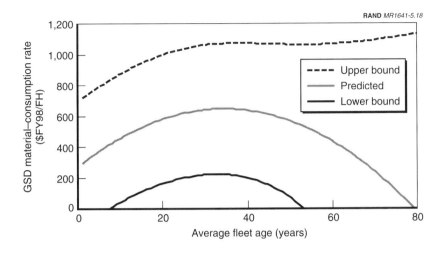

Figure 5.18—The GSD Consumption of More-Expensive Cargo Aircraft
Becomes Highly Unpredictable After Age 40

FINDINGS FOR REPLACEMENT SUPPORT EQUIPMENT EXPENDITURES

In Table 5.19, which shows the parameter coefficient estimates for
the full regression of costs for replacement support equipment as
aircraft fleets age, we can see that the full regression found that the
pure age (FAge) and age–flyaway cost interaction (FAge*Fly) terms
significantly affect annual equipment purchases per aircraft. In addition, it found that bomber (Bmbr), cargo (Crgo), and electronic
command and control (C2) aircraft generally have higher annual
support equipment replacement costs (after accounting for flyaway
cost and age), and that helicopters (Helo) and tankers (Tnkr) have
lower costs.

Table 5.19

Age Affects Replacement Equipment Purchases in the Full Regression

Results of regression analysis
Analysis Performed: Sun 03 Nov 2002 13:32:25
Data set used: D:\Documents\Dbases\Analysis\DataFiles\Equip98
Rule set used:
D:\Documents\Dbases\Analysis\Rules\EquipRules3

Dependent variable:	LEquip
Total sum of squares	4.6138E+11
Regression sum of squares	4.0787E+11
Residual error	5.6689E+10
F-Statistic	46.5268
Degrees of freedom	15,97
R-squared	0.8780

Variable	Coefficient	Standard Error	t-Statistic	Probability
Constant	4.18E+04			
Bmbr	7.17E+04	1.55E+04	4.6200	7.47E-05
C2	6.00E+04	9291.0973	6.4592	2.28E-06
Crgo	2.92E+04	6938.4930	4.2098	1.88E-04
Helo	−2.73E+04	1.09E+04	−2.4950	0.0137
OSA	−1.73E+04	9446.5821	−1.8333	0.0663
Tnkr	−4.07E+04	1.18E+04	−0.1408	1.19E-03
Trnr	−1403.0281	9967.9680	−3.4498	0.8833
FAge	−684.4879	306.1021	−2.2361	0.0260
Flyaway	33.4582	35.9263	0.9313	0.6435
Year98	−1713.4873	2458.5103	−0.6970	0.5054
FAge*Fly	28.7779	4.1336	6.9619	1.03E-06
Pulse5	9677.6728	3.25E+04	0.2981	0.7639
Pulse10	1.01E+04	1.74E+04	0.5790	0.5710
Ramp5	−1.53E+04	5.74E+04	−0.2662	0.7860
Ramp10	−7.09E+04	7.91E+04	−0.8969	0.6246

A Stepwise Backward Regression Reduced the Independent Variables

We used a stepwise backward regression to eliminate the nonsignificant regression variables progressively, one at a time, until all coefficients had probabilities of .05 or less. Table 5.20 displays the final results of that process.

Table 5.20

Age Affects Replacement Equipment Purchases in the Reduced Regression

Results of regression analysis
Analysis Performed: Sun 03 Nov 2002 13:35:36
Data set used:
D:\Documents\Dbases\Analysis\DataFiles\Equip98
Rule set used:
D:\Documents\Dbases\Analysis\Rules\EquipRules3

Dependent variable:	LEquip
Total sum of squares	4.6456E+11
Regression sum of squares	4.0544E+11
Residual error	5.9116E+10
F-Statistic	78.4906
Degrees of freedom	9,103
R-squared	0.8727

Variable	Coefficient	Standard Error	t-Statistic	Probability
Constant	4.20E+04			
Bmbr	7.73E+04	1.47E+04	5.2501	1.95E-05
C2	5.93E+04	8370.1321	7.0823	8.19E-07
Crgo	2.92E+04	6263.4956	4.6560	6.72E-05
Helo	−2.58E+04	1.06E+04	−2.4416	0.0155
OSA	−1.85E+04	8528.8319	−2.1702	0.0303
Tnkr	−4.12E+04	1.10E+04	−3.7387	5.68E-04
FAge	−880.5757	250.3005	−3.5181	9.84E-04
FAge*Fly	32.1931	2.8076	11.4662	5.76E-09
Ramp10	−5.57E+04	1.32E+04	−4.2071	1.85E-04

We can see that all the variables that were significant in the full regression remained significant in the reduced equation. In addition, the operations support aircraft (OSA) variable and the 10-year diminishing-ramp variable (Ramp10) emerged as significant in the reduced equation.

No Deceleration Was Found in Replacement Support Equipment Purchases

As shown in Table 5.21, when the second-order growth term $FAge20^2$ was added to the reduced equation, the regression did not find it significant beyond the .05 level. Presumably, the equation without the second-order term predicts the likely requirement for equipment purchases as accurately as the second-order equation, at least for the range of the data available for this study. Therefore, we examined the linear equation whose parameters are shown in Table 5.20 more closely.

First, we examined Cook's distance and leverage values in a scatterplot and found that all data points were within acceptable levels for Cook's distance. Thus, there is no evidence that a small subset of data points unduly influenced the results.

Table 5.21

Deceleration in Replacement Equipment Purchases Was Not Significant

Results of regression analysis
Analysis Performed: Sun 03 Nov 2002 13:36:48
Data set used:
D:\Documents\Dbases\Analysis\DataFiles\Equip98
Rule set used:
D:\Documents\Dbases\Analysis\Rules\EquipRules33

Dependent variable:	LEquip	
Total sum of squares	4.6456E+11	
Regression sum of squares	4.0643E+11	
Residual error	5.8126E+10	
F-Statistic	71.3218	
Degrees of freedom	10,102	
R-squared	0.8749	

Variable	Coefficient	Standard Error	t-Statistic	Probability
Constant	4.67E+04			
Bmbr	7.05E+04	1.54E+04	4.5859	7.90E-05
C2	5.80E+04	8399.4875	6.9013	1.09E-06
Crgo	2.75E+04	6360.4247	4.3309	1.39E-04
Helo	−2.73E+04	1.06E+04	−2.5790	0.0110
OSA	−1.76E+04	8527.7737	−2.0612	0.0393
Tnkr	−4.74E+04	1.19E+04	−3.9681	3.26E-04
FAge	−1316.1439	413.9309	−3.1796	2.33E-03
FAge*Fly	33.2032	2.9006	11.4469	5.95E-09
FAge20^2	47.3550	35.9162	1.3185	0.1872
Ramp10	−8.02E+04	2.28E+04	−3.5170	9.89E-04

Practical Implications of the Regression Equation

In Figure 5.19, which displays the forecasts for the reduced equation's support equipment requirements for the $30-million fighter and the $100-million cargo aircraft fleets, we can see that the replacement equipment expenditures for the cargo aircraft grow much faster than those for the fighter. Indeed, the fighter's equipment requirements hardly grow at all, because the age–flyaway cost interaction term is only slightly larger than the negative basic age effect. That is, the age–flyaway cost interaction growth is (30 * 32.1931 = 966.793), which is only slightly more than 880.5757 in Table 5.20. In contrast, the equipment purchase requirements for the $100-million cargo aircraft grow much more rapidly because the age–flyaway cost interaction term dominates the negative basic age effect.

As we can see in Figure 5.20, which shows the effect of aircraft age on the range of likely expenditures for replacement support equipment for the $30-million fighter and in Figure 5.21 for the $100-million

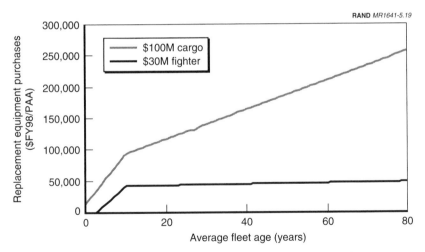

Figure 5.19—More-Expensive Aircraft Experience Greater Replacement-Equipment Cost Growth

cargo aircraft, the range of likely expenditures fans out as the aircraft age increases.

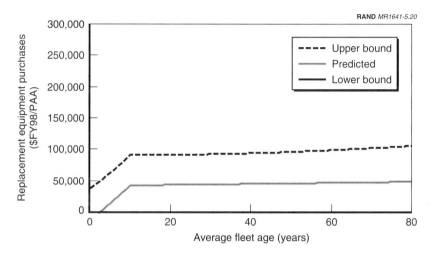

Figure 5.20—Forecast Requirements for Fighters' Replacement Support Equipment Become Less Predictable After Age 30

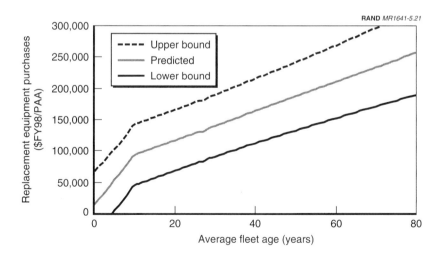

Figure 5.21—Forecast Requirements for Cargo Aircraft Fleets' Replacement Equipment Become Less Predictable After Age 40

FINDINGS FOR PROGRAMMED DEPOT MAINTENANCE WORKLOADS

Table 5.22 shows the parameter coefficient estimates for the full regression of programmed depot maintenance (PDM) costs as aircraft fleets age. The full regression found a statistically significant relationship between both the lead-age variable ("LdAge") and the lead-age–flyaway cost interaction ("LdAge*Fly"). It also found a signifi-

Table 5.22

Pure Lead Fleet Age and Lead Fleet Age Versus Flyaway Cost Significantly Affected Programmed Depot Maintenance Workloads in the Full Regression

Results of regression analysis				
Analysis Performed: Mon 18 Mar 2002 15:27:34				
Data set used: D:\Documents\Dbases\Analysis\DataFiles\PDM				
Rule set used: D:\Documents\Dbases\Analysis\Rules\PDMRules				
Dependent variable:	LWork			
Total sum of squares	6.1076E+09			
Regression sum of squares	4.9157E+09			
Residual error	1.1918E+09			
F-Statistic	39.5265			
Degrees of freedom	12,115			
R-squared	0.8049			

Variable	Coefficient	Standard Error	t-Statistic	Probability
Constant	1.14E+04			
B52	1.27E+04	4460.9941	2.8357	0.0056
C5	1.20E+04	1.31E+04	0.9149	0.6349
C130	−4682.1963	1524.6437	−3.0710	3.02E-03
C135	−6143.1020	2501.2989	−2.4560	0.0148
C141	−1975.2224	2819.3846	−0.7006	0.5079
Flyaway	−188.4999	105.3670	−1.7890	0.0726
Year92	−84.1823	196.7599	−0.4278	0.6734
LdAge	511.9739	93.6886	5.4646	1.21E-05
Period	−938.6825	774.2737	−1.2123	0.2257
Follow	−358.1684	174.1065	−2.0572	0.0394
LdAge*Fly	7.4272	1.4397	5.1589	2.21E-05
Fol*Fly	0.2886	1.2151	0.2375	0.8078

cant effect for the age difference between the oldest MDS in an MD and the following MDS's age ("Follow"). It did not find the basic fly-away cost ("Flyaway"), the inter-PDM interval ("Period"), the calendar effect ("Year92"), or the interaction between the following MDS age and its cost ("Fol*Fly") significant. It also found that the B-52 had significantly higher PDM workloads than fighters (after flyaway cost has been considered), and that the C-135s and C-130s had significantly lower PDM workloads. It did not find that the C-5 or C-141 had higher workloads that were not explainable by differences in flyaway costs.

A Stepwise Backward Regression Reduced the Independent Variables

We used a stepwise backward regression to eliminate the nonsignificant regression variables progressively, one at a time, until all coefficients had probabilities of .05 or less. Table 5.23 displays the final results from that process.

We can see that all the variables that were statistically significant in the initial full regression remained significant in the reduced equation. Two new terms emerged as significant as the linear equation was reduced: the pure flyaway cost and the PDM period. Note that the equation indicates that C-130s and C-135s have substantially smaller workloads than the F-15. If all cargo aircraft, including the C-5 and C-141, had significantly smaller workloads, we might be tempted to suggest that cargo aircraft in general have smaller per-PDM workloads than do fighters and bombers. However, the available data do not include enough different fighter, bomber, and cargo platforms to draw that conclusion.

Table 5.23

Pure Lead Fleet Age and Lead Fleet Age Versus Flyaway Cost Significantly Affected Programmed Depot Maintenance Workloads in the Reduced Regression

Results of regression analysis
Analysis Performed: Mon 18 Mar 2002 15:29:49
Data set used: D:\Documents\Dbases\Analysis\DataFiles\PDM
Rule set used: D:\Documents\Dbases\Analysis\Rules\PDMRules

Dependent variable:	LWork			
Total sum of squares	6.1076E+09			
Regression sum of squares	4.9047E+09			
Residual error	1.2029E+09			
F-Statistic	60.6537			
Degrees of freedom	8,119			
R-squared	0.8031			

Variable	Coefficient	Standard Error	t-Statistic	Probability
Constant	1.07E+04			
B52	9729.7407	2477.6334	3.9270	3.44E-04
C130	–3587.8790	1004.1058	–3.5732	8.27E-04
C135	–7462.1702	1107.4666	–6.7381	1.25E-06
Flyaway	–95.3301	30.0959	–3.1675	2.34E-03
LdAge	486.8803	76.6697	6.3504	2.37E-06
Period	–1175.5401	555.4993	–2.1162	0.0342
Follow	–452.1490	81.1591	–5.5711	9.65E-06
LdAge*Fly	7.4697	1.3747	5.4338	1.26E-05

The Regression Found Significant Second-Order Acceleration in Late-Life Programmed Depot Maintenance Workloads

As shown in Table 5.24, the regression found a second-order growth effect centered on age 20, the LdAge20^2 factor, to be significant beyond the .05 level when added to the reduced equation. Presumably, the equation with the second-order term predicts the likely requirement for PDM workloads more accurately than does the linear equation alone, at least for the range of the data available for this study. Therefore, we examined more closely the second-order equation whose parameters are shown in Table 5.24.

Table 5.24

Programmed Depot Maintenance Workloads Significantly
Accelerated with Age in the Regression

Results of regression analysis
Analysis Performed: Mon 18 Mar 2002 15:30:46
Data set used: D:\Documents\Dbases\Analysis\DataFiles\PDM
Rule set used: D:\Documents\Dbases\Analysis\Rules\PDMRules

Dependent variable:	LWork			
Total sum of squares	6.1076E+09			
Regression sum of squares	5.1968E+09			
Residual error	9.1082E+08			
F-Statistic	74.8065			
Degrees of freedom	9,118			
R-squared	0.8509			

Variable	Coefficient	Standard Error	t-Statistic	Probability
Constant	1.33E+04			
B52	9974.2696	2165.4690	4.6061	7.09E-05
C130	−2577.9587	892.6770	−2.8879	4.85E-03
C135	−7968.7554	971.2685	−8.2045	1.52E-07
Flyaway	−111.3170	26.4277	−4.2121	1.74E-04
LdAge	301.2649	73.4808	4.0999	2.27E-04
Period	−1275.8498	485.7024	−2.6268	0.0095
Follow	−424.2231	71.0668	−5.9694	4.63E-06
LdAge*Fly	8.5720	1.2146	7.0576	7.63E-07
LdAge20^2	26.2593	4.2691	6.1510	3.35E-06

Practical Implications of the Regression Equation

Figure 5.22 displays the reduced second-order equation's workload
per-PDM visit forecasts for the $30-million fighter and the $100-
million cargo aircraft fleets. In contrast to the life-cycle patterns for
other workloads and material categories, the PDM workload displays
a pronounced acceleration as fleets age. Although the expensive
cargo fleet's PDM workloads are initially lower than the fighter

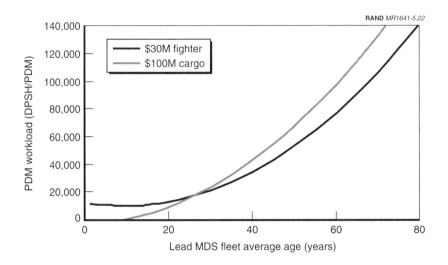

**Figure 5.22—Cargo Aircraft PDM Workloads Start Lower, but Grow Faster
Than Fighter Workloads**

fleet's, its basic growth rate is much higher, owing to the age–flyaway cost interaction. Thus, the cargo aircraft's PDM workloads catch and surpass the fighter's between ages 20 and 30 years. After that, the cargo aircraft workload grows even faster.

In Figure 5.23, which shows how aircraft age affects the (95-percent-confidence) range of likely per-PDM workloads for the $30-million fighter and in Figure 5.24 for the $100-million cargo aircraft, we can see that the range of likely expenditures clearly fans out as the aircraft age increases. Even more interesting, the figures indicate that the early-life range is also larger than the mid-life (ages 20–40) range.

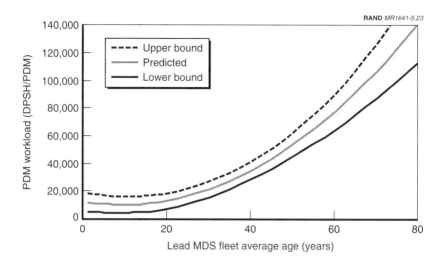

Figure 5.23—Fighter PDM Workloads Are Less Predictable in Both
Early-Life and Late-Life Periods

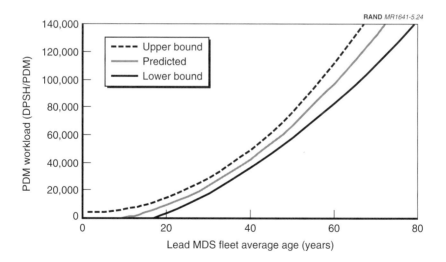

Figure 5.24—Cargo Aircraft PDM Workloads Are Also Less Predictable in
Both Early-Life and Late-Life Periods

Lead Fleet Age, Follow, and Intra-Mission-Design Learning

The significance of the variable "Follow" is that it suggests that younger fleets' PDM workloads are increased by "lessons learned" from experience with the older fleets of the same basic design. Follow is computed as the number of years between a given MDS's average fleet age and the age of the oldest MDS with the same mission design (MD). For example, the F-15 MD includes the F-15A, F-15B, F-15C, F-15D, and F-15E series, and each fleet has a different average age. All five fleets receive their PDMs at the same facility, using the same personnel, equipment, and material. The planning and engineering assessments of the fleet that underlie the PDM workload are carried out by the same engineering and maintenance planning personnel, and the workloads for each MDS's planned workload are negotiated and approved by the same MAJCOM representatives and PDM managers at the same Material Requirements Review Board.

As a consequence, participants on both sides learn a great deal about what workloads may arise during their support of the earlier MDS. (For example, many problems that emerge on the F-15A/B may be encountered on the later-produced F-15C/D/E models.) Recognizing that, the MRRB engineers, planners, and customers use the experience from the earlier model to guide their workload negotiations for the later series. To the extent that unexpected maintenance requirements are discovered during the lead fleet's PDMs, later fleets' PDM packages may include additional tasks to ensure that the potential material requirements are covered. As a consequence, the following fleets' PDM workloads at a given age tend to be higher than the lead fleet's at the same age.

The Follow variable captures that effect. In essence, the equation was constructed by assuming that similar fleets might be purchased in sequence over many years. If so, later fleets' workloads would reflect lessons learned during earlier fleets' PDMs. Then, the coefficient for the Follow variable in Table 5.24 tells us that the younger fleets' PDMs would require about 424 fewer depot product standard hours' work than the lead fleet for each year they trail the lead fleet in age. That is, the younger fleets need less work in the same year, but they will require more work when they reach the same age.

The Counterintuitive PDM Interval Effect

Engineering and maintenance experts may find the negative relationship between Period and workload surprising. Common sense and years of experience suggest that increasing the period between major heavy maintenance inspections should lead to the emergence of more material discrepancies, such as fatigue cracks and corrosion, and to the worsening of the original discrepancies. We can wonder, therefore, why the regression found that aircraft with longer intervals have smaller PDM workloads.

One possible reason may be that the Air Force does not lengthen the intervals on fleets whose material, design features, or usage patterns generate a substantial amount of maintenance work. That is, only the most reliable, maintainable and flight-safe aircraft may have their initial PDM interval lengthened as the Air Force engineering and maintenance establishments gain confidence in the aircraft structure and functional reliability. Indeed, many long-lived fleets have participated in a controlled interval-extension program that monitors the workload growth and the airworthiness of the aircraft as the PDM interval is extended.

A Possible Alternative Explanation and Prediction of the PDM Workload Acceleration

In Chapter Three, we hypothesized that major structural problems might emerge increasingly more rapidly as aircraft approach their designed service life, but then level off as inspections begin to cover most of the aircraft and repairs put some problems to rest. If so, it is possible that PDM workloads are composed of two different components, a relatively small but stable inspection workload, which grows slowly throughout the aircraft's life cycle, and a larger workload, which emerges late in the life cycle, say, as the aircraft approaches the design life. If that were indeed the case, the second-order equation based only on that early experience would overestimate the workload growth in later life, because the early- to mid-life acceleration would not continue.

The linear extrapolation might also overestimate future growth, but it would not forecast the extraordinarily large late-life workloads forecast by the second-order equation, as shown in Figure 5.25. We

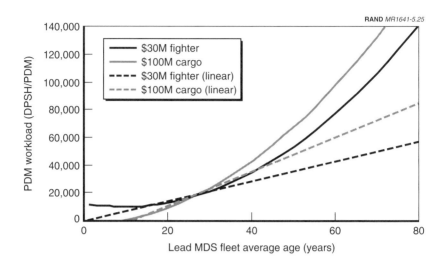

**Figure 5.25—The Linear Equation Forecasts Lower Workload Growth
After Age 30**

can see from the figure that the two forecasting equations agree fairly well for the period between ages 10 and 35 (where most of the historical data originate) but diverge strongly at higher ages. If the second-order effect is caused by the late-life emergence of DSO inspection and repair workloads, as suggested in Chapter Three, both forecasts may overestimate future workload sizes.

Only time and experience with older aircraft will clarify this issue. Over the next decade or two, the Air Force will gain experience with operating aircraft in those extended-life periods, and it will be possible to estimate future PDM workloads more accurately. Until then, these two divergent forecasts may be useful for forecasting a few years past that range, but longer forecasts will not reflect the natural limits to workload growth suggested in Chapter Three.

FINDINGS FOR ENGINE OVERHAUL WORKLOADS

Table 5.25 shows the parameter coefficient estimates for the full regression of annual engine-overhaul workloads as aircraft fleets age. As discussed in Chapter Four, pure jet engines with no fan and no augmentor but with a scheduled overhaul were used as the reference set. Then, categorical variables were included for engines with turbofans, augmentors (i.e., afterburner stage), engines with no scheduled depot overhaul, the F100 engine design, and the F110 enginedesign. (There were no data for engine fleets averaging less than five years old, so break-in variables were included only for the 10-year pulse and 10-year ramp.) Continuous variables were

Table 5.25

Age Did Not Significantly Affect Engine-Overhaul Costs in the Full Regression

Results of regression analysis
Analysis Performed: Wed 06 Mar 2002 16:02:31
Data set used:
D:\Documents\Dbases\Analysis\DataFiles\EngineOH
Rule set used:
D:\Documents\Dbases\Analysis\Rules\EngOHRules

Dependent variable:	EstAnnual
Total sum of squares	22.0137
Regression sum of squares	13.0051
Residual error	9.0086
F-Statistic	3.8060
Degrees of freedom	11,29
R-squared	0.5908

Variable	Coefficient	Standard Error	t-Statistic	Probability
Constant	−1.2976			
F100	−0.2267	0.5201	−0.4359	0.6697
F110	0.7660	0.3919	1.9544	0.0574
EAge	0.0148	0.0512	0.2887	0.7717
EWeight	2.42E-04	3.42E-04	0.7085	0.5090
Year98	−0.0977	0.1967	−0.4966	0.6286
EAge* EWeight	1.27E-05	1.31E-05	0.9659	0.6561
Fan	−1.2005	0.7621	−1.5752	0.1225
Aug	1.2406	0.2920	4.2489	3.95E-04
NoOH	0.4008	0.5006	0.8005	0.5645
EPulse10	0.0663	1.3394	0.0495	0.9598
ERamp10	−0.1120	5.9102	−0.0189	0.9826

included for engine weight, average engine fleet age, and the interaction (product) of age and engine weight.

As can be seen in Table 5.25, the regression found that engines with an augmentor ("Aug") required higher depot-level overhaul workloads per engine flying hour than did other engines. No other variables were significant in the full regression.

A Stepwise Backward Regression Reduced the Independent Variables

We used a stepwise backward regression to eliminate the nonsignificant regression variables progressively, one at a time, until all coefficients had probabilities of .05 or less. Table 5.26 displays the final results from that process.

The augmentor variable remains significant in the reduced equation. In addition, the fan and F110 categorical variables and the age-weight interaction term emerge as significant in the reduced equation.

The Regression Detected No Second-Order Deceleration in Engine-Overhaul Workloads

As shown in Table 5.27, the regression did not find the second-order growth term centered on age 20 to be significant beyond the .05 level when it was added to the reduced equations. Presumably, the equation without the second-order term predicts the requirement for engine overhaul as accurately as the second-order equation, at least for the range of data available for this study. Therefore, we examined more closely the linear equation whose parameters are shown in Table 5.25.

First, we examined the Cook's distance and leverage values in a scatterplot and we found that all data points were within acceptable levels for Cook's distance.

Table 5.26

Age Versus Engine Weight Significantly Affected Engine-Overhaul Costs in the Reduced Linear Regression

Results of regression analysis
Analysis Performed: Wed 06 Mar 2002 16:04:42
Data set used:
D:\Documents\Dbases\Analysis\DataFiles\EngineOH
Rule set used:
D:\Documents\Dbases\Analysis\Rules\EngOHRules

Dependent variable:	EstAnnual			
Total sum of squares	22.0137			
Regression sum of squares	11.9214			
Residual error	10.0923			
F-Statistic	10.6311			
Degrees of freedom	4,36			
R-squared	0.5415			

Variable	Coefficient	Standard Error	t-Statistic	Probability
Constant	−0.6426			
F110	0.9963	0.2548	3.9102	6.47E-04
EAge* EWeight	1.62E-05	3.04E-06	5.3201	4.33E-05
Fan	−0.9111	0.3353	−2.7175	0.0098
Aug	1.1034	0.2536	4.3510	2.59E-04

Practical Implications of the Reduced Equation

As shown in Figure 5.26, the regression forecasts a rising requirement for depot engine overhauls as engine fleets age. (The workloads depicted represent the work per engine flying hour for a 3,700-lb augmented fan engine on a fighter and 5,000-lb unaugmented fan engine on a cargo aircraft.)

As we can see from the figure, the larger engine on the cargo aircraft has very low workloads for the first 20 or so years, but its workload grows much faster after that point. (The regression equation actually computes large negative workloads at earlier ages, which is impossible, of course. Most likely, the initial overhaul workload is much lower than the later-life workload. If there had been more data available for younger engines, this regression might have found a signifi-

Table 5.27

Engine-Overhaul Costs Do Not Significantly Decelerate with Age

Results of regression analysis
Analysis Performed: Wed 06 Mar 2002 16:05:24
Data set used:
D:\Documents\Dbases\Analysis\DataFiles\EngineOH
Rule set used:
D:\Documents\Dbases\Analysis\Rules\EngOHRules

Dependent variable:	EstAnnual			
Total sum of squares	22.0137			
Regression sum of squares	11.9215			
Residual error	10.0922			
F-Statistic	8.2688			
Degrees of freedom	5,35			
R-squared	0.5415			

Variable	Coefficient	Standard Error	t-Statistic	Probability
Constant	−0.6396			
F110	0.9978	0.2742	3.6393	1.19E-03
EAge* EWeight	1.62E-05	3.67E-06	4.4066	2.39E-04
Fan	−0.9166	0.4800	−1.9094	0.0613
Aug	1.1044	0.2640	4.1838	3.74E-04
EAge20^2	−1.45E-05	8.83E-04	−0.0164	0.9843

cant second-order acceleration such as that found in the PDM analysis.)

In practical terms, a cargo aircraft's total engine-overhaul workload grows more than a fighter's, not only because each engine is heavier but because there are usually more engines per aircraft. As seen in the figure, the 5,000-lb engine grows only slightly faster than a fighter's 3,700-lb engine. Each 5,000-lb engine's workload would grow by (0.0000162 * 5000 = 0.084 DPSH per engine flying hour), which may still sound small. However, most cargo aircraft have two to four engines. Thus, each 4-engine cargo aircraft wing of 30 cargo aircraft flying 500 hours each per year would see its depot overhaul requirement grow (30 * 4 * 500 * 0.084 = 5,040 additional DPSH [about 3 depot technicians] per year) after age 20. In contrast, each fighter fleet would experience much smaller annual workload growth for three reasons:

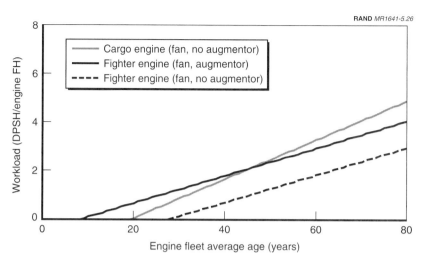

Figure 5.26—Workloads for Augmented Engines Are Higher, but Workloads for Heavier Engines Grow Faster

- Lower engine weight
- Fewer engines per aircraft
- Lower annual flying hours.

An individual 3,700-lb fighter engine would experience slightly less than three-fourths of the workload growth of its counterpart on a cargo aircraft, or 0.0599 DPSH per flying hour per year. While some fighters have two engines each, many have only one engine. Thus, a 54-aircraft fighter wing with single-engine aircraft each flying 300 flying hours per year would see its requirement for depot overhauls grow only 970 additional DPSH, or less than one additional depot maintenance technician per year.

The other point of interest in Figure 5.26 is that fighter engines with augmentors experience higher workloads than engines without augmentors. The higher workload reflects the influence of the aug-mentor categorical variable. The augmentor is used to boost power during combat maneuvers. Some combination of the more-frequent temperature swings, higher temperatures, higher g-forces, and higher vibrations may increase the annual depot-overhaul workload requirement for augmented fighter engines relative to that for nonaugmented engines.

How engine age affects the range of likely overhaul workloads is shown in Figure 5.27 for the augmented fighter engine and in Figure 5.28 for the cargo aircraft engine. The 95-percent confidence interval clearly fans out at both young and old ages, especially for the cargo engine (Figure 5.28). As with the anticipated fan-out at older ages, the fan-out at younger ages reflects the limited range of average ages available for engine fleets for this analysis.

COST FINDINGS FOR PER-AIRCRAFT CONTRACTOR LOGISTICS SUPPORT

Table 5.28 shows the parameter-coefficient estimates for the full regression of per-aircraft contractor logistics support (CLS) costs as aircraft fleets age. The full regression found a significant relationship between the age–flyaway cost interaction variable and per-aircraft CLS costs. No other terms were statistically significant.

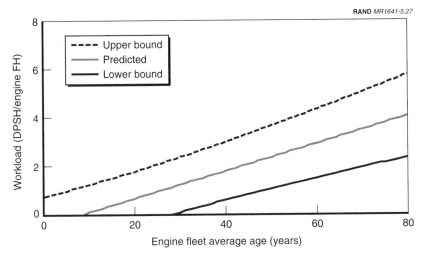

Figure 5.27—Predicted Variability for Fighter Engine Depot-Overhaul Workloads Increases as Fleets Age

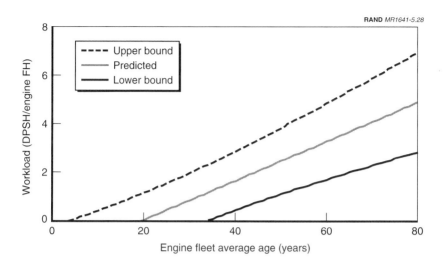

Figure 5.28— Predicted Variability for Cargo Aircraft Engine Depot-Overhaul Workloads Grows Also as Fleets Age

A Stepwise Backward Regression Reduced the Independent Variables

We used a stepwise backward regression to eliminate the nonsignificant regression variables progressively, one at a time, until all coefficients had probabilities of .05 or less. Table 5.29 displays the final results from that process.

We can see that the age–flyaway cost term remained significant and that the 5-year pulse break-in variable became significant as the other break-in terms were eliminated.

Table 5.28

Age Affected Per-Aircraft Contractor Logistics Support Costs in the Full Regression

Results of regression analysis
Analysis Performed: Tue 12 Nov 2002 15:32:34
Data set used:
D:\Documents\Dbases\Analysis\DataFiles\CLSAcft
Rule set used:
D:\Documents\Dbases\Analysis\Rules\CLSAcftRules

Dependent variable:	LCPA			
Total sum of squares	4.9053E+14			
Regression sum of squares	1.9662E+14			
Residual error	2.9391E+14			
F-Statistic	3.3449			
Degrees of freedom	8,40			
R-squared	0.4008			

Variable	Coefficient	Standard Error	t-Statistic	Probability
Constant	1.61E+06			
FAge	9075.8816	5.94E+04	0.1527	0.8740
Flyaway	−1389.0590	1.01E+04	0.1369	0.8868
FAge*Fly	1640.2519	554.2637	2.9593	0.0053
Pulse5	5.36E+06	4.61E+06	1.1630	0.2504
Pulse10	5.31E+06	6.24E+06	0.8515	0.5959
Ramp5	5.62E+06	1.05E+07	0.5368	0.6007
Ramp10	−1.47E+07	1.94E+07	−0.7573	0.5404
Year99	−1.19E+06	8.05E+05	−1.4836	0.1421

The Regression Detected No Per-Aircraft CLS Cost Deceleration

As shown in Table 5.30, the regression found that the second-order term for age-related growth in per-aircraft CLS costs, $FAge20^2$, was not significant beyond the .05 level when added to the reduced equation. Presumably, the equation without the second-order term predicts the requirement for annual per-aircraft CLS expenditures as accurately as the second-order equation, at least for the range of data available for this study. Therefore, we examined more closely the linear equation whose parameters are shown in Table 5.29.

Table 5.29

Age Affected Per-Aircraft Contractor Logistics Support Costs
in the Reduced Regression

Results of regression analysis				
Analysis Performed: Tue 12 Nov 2002 15:36:13				
Data set used:				
D:\Documents\Dbases\Analysis\DataFiles\CLSAcft				
Rule set used:				
D:\Documents\Dbases\Analysis\Rules\CLSAcftRules				
Dependent variable:	LCPA			
Total sum of squares	4.9053E+14			
Regression sum of squares	1.7349E+14			
Residual error	3.1704E+14			
F-Statistic	12.5859			
Degrees of freedom	2,46			
R-squared	0.3537			
Variable	Coefficient	Standard Error	*t*-Statistic	Probability
Constant	1.33E+06			
FAge*Fly	1692.6748	343.5233	4.9280	6.63E-05
Pulse5	2.02E+06	9.05E+05	2.2267	0.0291

First, we examined Cook's distance and leverage values were examined in a scatterplot, and we found that all data points were within acceptable levels for Cook's distance.

Even though the Cook's distance is well within acceptable levels, we should note that the vast majority of the CLS aircraft are either young or inexpensive. Only the E-4 aircraft was both expensive ($244-million flyaway cost) and over 20 years of age. Indeed that aircraft's data had the greatest leverage. However, a follow-up analysis confirmed that a backward stepwise regression with the E-4 data removed found that the same two independent variables were still significant. Therefore, the E-4 data were retained.

Table 5.30

Per-Aircraft Contractor Logistics Support Costs Did Not Decelerate

Results of regression analysis				
Analysis Performed: Tue 12 Nov 2002 15:37:23				
Data set used:				
D:\Documents\Dbases\Analysis\DataFiles\CLSAcft				
Rule set used:				
D:\Documents\Dbases\Analysis\Rules\CLSAcftRules				
Dependent variable:	LCPA			
Total sum of squares	4.9053E+14			
Regression sum of				
squares	1.7350E+14			
Residual error	3.1703E+14			
F-Statistic	8.2092			
Degrees of freedom	3,45			
R-squared	0.3537			
Variable	Coefficient	Standard Error	t-Statistic	Probability
Constant	1.35E+06			
FAge*Fly	1691.7322	348.2916	4.8572	7.76E-05
Pulse5	2.07E+06	1.46E+06	1.4142	0.1600
FAge20^2	–205.1284	4686.9129	–0.0438	0.9642

Practical Implications of the Reduced Equations

From the life-cycle CLS per-aircraft maintenance-cost projections for the two CLS aircraft in Figure 5.29—one costing $30 million and the other costing $100 million—we can see that both aircraft have about the same initial expected CLS cost per year, near $3.4 million. However, their costs begin to diverge almost immediately. The more-expensive aircraft's costs climb to over $4.0 million by age 4 while the less-expensive aircraft's costs have grown to only $3.6 million. At age 5, their annual costs drop substantially, but the gap continues to widen. By age 40, the more-expensive aircraft would cost over $8.1 million per year according to the regression equation; the less-expensive one would cost less than $3.4 million.

How aircraft age affects the range of likely annual per-aircraft CLS costs is shown in Figure 5.30 for the $30-million aircraft and in Figure 5.31 for the $100-million aircraft. The fan-out is apparent in both

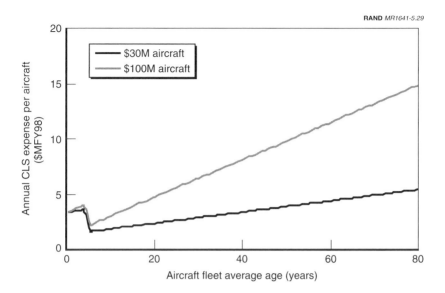

Figure 5.29—More-Expensive Aircraft Experience Faster Growth in CLS
Cost per Aircraft

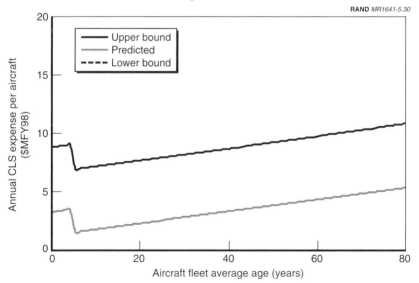

Figure 5.30—Less-Expensive Aircraft CLS Costs per Aircraft May Vary
Widely

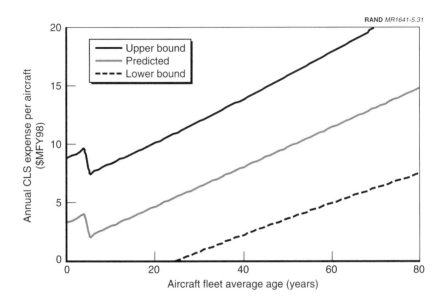

Figure 5.31—More-Expensive Aircraft CLS Costs per Aircraft May Vary Even More Widely Than Those for Less-Expensive Aircraft

figures. Note that the size of the 95-percent confidence interval is greater than the expected value of CLS cost for most of both fleets' service lives. This suggests that even though age affects CLS costs, so do many other factors that have not been discovered in this analysis.

COST FINDINGS FOR PER-FLYING-HOUR CONTRACTOR LOGISTICS SUPPORT

Table 5.31 shows the parameter-coefficient estimates for the full regression of per-flying-hour contractor logistics support (CLS) charges as aircraft fleets age. Because so few early-life data points were available, we eliminated the two break-in ramp variables. Indeed, a series of tests with all four break-in variables revealed that at least one had to be removed to eliminate their mutual redundancy.

Table 5.31

Age Affects Per-Flying-Hour Contractor Logistics Support Costs
in the Full Regression

Results of regression analysis
Analysis Performed: Tue 12 Nov 2002 17:00:18
Data set used: D:\Documents\Dbases\Analysis\DataFiles\CLSFH
Rule set used:
D:\Documents\Dbases\Analysis\Rules\CLSFHRules

Dependent variable:	LCPFH
Total sum of squares	6.5783E+05
Regression sum of squares	4.8180E+05
Residual error	1.7603E+05
F-Statistic	5.9303
Degrees of freedom	6,13
R-squared	0.7324

Variable	Coefficient	Standard Error	t-Statistic	Probability
Constant	242.4878			
FAge	–3.8692	3.8721	–0.9992	0.6627
Flyaway	1.1057	0.6522	1.6954	0.1108
FAge*Fly	0.2568	0.0906	2.8358	0.0135
Pulse5	150.3377	137.9003	1.0902	0.2957
Pulse10	–133.2674	147.1331	–0.9058	0.6151
Year99	–11.3191	56.2819	–0.2011	0.8376

As can be seen in the table, the age–flyaway cost interaction term significantly affected the per-flying-hour CLS costs. No other factors were significant.

A Stepwise Backward Regression Reduced the Independent Variables

We used a stepwise backward regression to eliminate the nonsignificant regression variables progressively, one at a time, until all coefficients had probabilities of .05 or less. Table 5.32 displays the final results from that process.

We can see in the table that the age–flyaway cost interaction term remained significant and that the flyaway cost emerged as significant.

Table 5.32

Age Affects Per-Flying-Hour Contractor Logistics Support Costs in the Reduced Regression

Results of regression analysis
Analysis Performed: Tue 12 Nov 2002 17:03:12
Data set used: D:\Documents\Dbases\Analysis\DataFiles\CLSFH
Rule set used:
D:\Documents\Dbases\Analysis\Rules\CLSFHRules

Dependent variable:	LnCPFH			
Total sum of squares	6.5783E+05			
Regression sum of squares	4.3824E+05			
Residual error	2.1959E+05			
F-Statistic	16.9638			
Degrees of freedom	2,17			
R-squared	0.6662			
Variable	Coefficient	Standard Error	t-Statistic	Probability
Constant	156.4790			
Flyaway	1.5835	0.5034	3.1452	0.0060
FAge*Fly	0.2282	0.0729	3.1318	0.0061

As shown in Table 5.33, the regression found that the Age20^2 factor was not significant beyond the .05 level when added to the reduced equation, so no significant deceleration occurs in per-flying-hour CLS costs. Presumably, the equation without the second-order term predicts the requirement for annual per-aircraft CLS expenditures as accurately as the second-order equation, at least for the range of data available for this study. Therefore, we examined more closely the linear equation whose parameters are shown in Table 5.32.

First, we examined Cook's distance and leverage values in a scatter-plot, and we found that the single available point for the E-9A aircraft (in 1999) was at the high end of the leverage scale; its Cook's distance was near 9.

Table 5.33

Per-Flying-Hour Contractor Logistics Support Costs Do Not Decelerate

Results of regression analysis				
Analysis Performed: Tue 12 Nov 2002 17:04:24				
Data set used: D:\Documents\Dbases\Analysis\DataFiles\CLSFH				
Rule set used:				
D:\Documents\Dbases\Analysis\Rules\CLSFHRules				
Dependent variable:	LnCPFH			
Total sum of squares	6.5783E+05			
Regression sum of squares	4.3922E+05			
Residual error	2.1862E+05			
F-Statistic	10.7151			
Degrees of freedom	3,16			
R-squared	0.6677			

Variable	Coefficient	Standard Error	t-Statistic	Probability
Constant	165.2938			
Flyaway	1.6502	0.5749	2.8705	0.0108
FAge*Fly	0.2178	0.0844	2.5803	0.0192
FAge20^2	−0.0582	0.2180	−0.2671	0.7884

A Cook's distance greater than 1.0 is usually regarded as a concern that the results may be distorted, especially when the same point has high leverage. Removing the data point from the backward stepwise regression analysis yielded a simpler reduced equation with only the age–flyaway cost term indicated as being statistically significant, as shown in Table 5.34.

Comparing the results from Table 5.32 with those of Table 5.34, we can see that the E-9A's presence contributes substantially to the significance of the flyaway-cost term in Table 5.32. More interesting, removing that data point causes the estimated age–flyaway cost coefficient to increase by over 40 percent. The E-9A costs $244 million, and the next-most-expensive aircraft (the KC-10A) costs only $88 million. After that, the remaining aircraft cost less than 10 percent of the E-9A flyaway cost. Clearly, the E-9A has a relatively high per-flying-hour CLS cost at a relatively young age, a cost so high that it may distort the size of the age–flyaway cost interaction term.

Table 5.34

Age Still Affects Per-Flying-Hour Contractor Logistics Support Costs in the Reduced Regression with E-9A Data Removed

Results of regression analysis
Analysis Performed: Mon 25 Nov 2002 12:10:39
Data set used:
D:\Documents\Dbases\Analysis\DataFiles\CLSFHNoE9
Rule set used:
D:\Documents\Dbases\Analysis\Rules\CLSFHRules

Dependent variable:	LnCPFH			
Total sum of squares	5.4482E+05			
Regression sum of squares	3.1309E+05			
Residual error	2.3173E+05			
F-Statistic	22.9685			
Degrees of freedom	1,17			
R-squared	0.5747			

Variable	Coefficient	Standard Error	t-Statistic	Probability
Constant	157.8005			
FAge*Fly	0.3257	0.0680	4.7926	3.32E-04

There is no evidence that the E-9A per-flying-hour CLS maintenance cost is inaccurate in any way. Its maintenance costs may typify those of more-expensive aircraft, even at an early age. Absent additional data for other expensive aircraft, its data were retained for this analysis.

Practical Implications of the Reduced Equations

Figure 5.32 shows the forecast per-flying-hour CLS costs for two aircraft, one costing $30 million and the other costing $100 million. Themore-expensive aircraft's costs start $100 per flying hour higher than the less-expensive aircraft's. From that point, the more-expensive aircraft's costs climb nearly three times as fast. In contrast to most other cost or workload categories, no break-in effects are apparent, but that may be due to the small sample size.

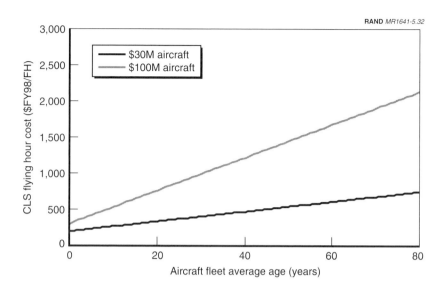

Figure 5.32—Per-Flying-Hour Charges for Contractor Logistics Support Increase over First Ten Years of Service Life

How aircraft age affects the range of likely annual per-flying-hour CLS costs is shown in Figure 5.33 for the $30-million aircraft and in Figure 5.34 for the $100-million aircraft. The fan-out in these figures is more clearly observed than in most of the analyses in this study.

FINDINGS FOR DLR MODERNIZATION

Table 5.35 shows the parameter-coefficient estimates for the full regression of depot-level reparable (DLR) component purchases as aircraft fleets age. Age, flyaway cost, and their interaction were all significant in the full regressions, as are the 5-year break-in ramp variable and the electronic command and control categorical variable.

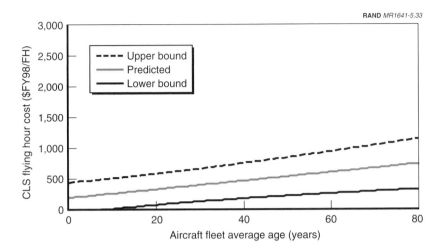

**Figure 5.33—Prediction Uncertainties for Contractor Logistics Support
Per-Flying-Hour Costs Increase for Older, Less-Expensive Aircraft**

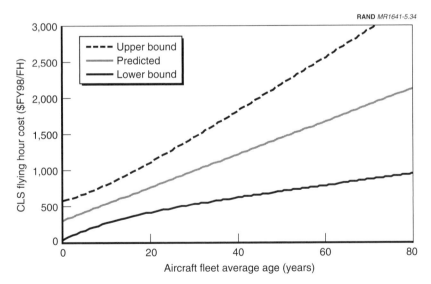

**Figure 5.34—Prediction Uncertainties for Contractor Logistics Support
Per-Flying-Hour Costs Increase Even Faster for More-Expensive Aircraft**

Table 5.35

Age Affected Depot-Level Reparable Purchases in the Full Regression

Results of regression analysis
Analysis Performed: Mon 18 Mar 2002 17:55:35
Data set used:
D:\Documents\Dbases\Analysis\DataFiles\ConsDLRBuy$
Rule set used:
D:\Documents\Dbases\Analysis\Rules\ConsDLRBuyRules

Dependent variable:	LInvest			
Total sum of squares	4.5430			
Regression sum of squares	3.4018			
Residual error	1.1412			
F-Statistic	17.1979			
Degrees of freedom	13,75			
R-squared	0.7488			

Variable	Coefficient	Standard Error	t-Statistic	Probability
Constant	0.1092			
Bmbr	0.0482	0.0824	0.5846	0.5676
C2	0.2042	0.0789	2.5872	0.0112
Crgo	−0.0632	0.0652	−0.9690	0.6628
Helo	0.0491	0.0456	1.0775	0.2845
Trnr	0.0776	0.0698	1.1116	0.2691
FAge	−0.0062	2.47E-03	−2.5243	0.0131
Flyaway	−8.57E-04	2.34E-04	−3.6567	7.70E-04
Year98	0.0065	0.0085	0.7677	0.5487
FAge*Fly	2.24E-04	3.52E-05	6.3529	3.39E-06
Pulse5	−0.0629	0.1679	−0.3748	0.7102
Pulse10	−0.0676	0.0827	−0.8177	0.5786
Ramp5	1.0331	0.3054	3.3827	1.51E-03
Ramp10	0.0418	0.2661	0.1571	0.8701

A Stepwise Backward Regression Reduced the Independent Variables

As with the other analyses, we used a stepwise backward regression to eliminate the nonsignificant regression variables progressively, one at a time, until all coefficients had probabilities of .05 or less. Table 5.36 displays the final results from that process.

All the variables that were significant in the full regression remained significant in the reduced equation. In addition, the reduced regression identified cargo aircraft as having significantly lower DLR purchases than most other aircraft.

Table 5.36

Age Affected Depot-Level Reparable Purchases in the Reduced Regression

Results of regression analysis
Analysis Performed: Mon 18 Mar 2002 17:59:07
Data set used:
D:\Documents\Dbases\Analysis\DataFiles\ConsDLRBuy$
Rule set used:
D:\Documents\Dbases\Analysis\Rules\ConsDLRBuyRules

Dependent variable:	LInvest			
Total sum of squares	4.5430			
Regression sum of squares	3.3537			
Residual error	1.1893			
F-Statistic	38.5391			
Degrees of freedom	6,82			
R-squared	0.7382			

Variable	Coefficient	Standard Error	t-Statistic	Probability
Constant	0.0703			
C2	0.1776	0.0575	3.0870	3.10E-03
Crgo	−0.1113	0.0354	−3.1409	2.71E-03
FAge	−3.70E-03	1.60E-03	−2.3053	0.0223
Flyaway	−8.98E-04	1.55E-04	−5.7794	8.31E-06
FAge*Fly	2.31E-04	2.28E-05	10.1428	2.73E-08
Ramp5	1.0305	0.2341	4.4027	1.31E-04

The Regression Detected No Per-Aircraft DLR Modernization Deceleration

As shown in Table 5.37, the regression found that the $FAge20^2$ factor was not significant beyond the .05 level when added to the reduced equation, so no significant second-order age-related growth occurs in DLR modernization costs. Presumably, the equation without the

Table 5.37

Depot-Level-Reparable Purchases Did Not Decelerate with Age in the Linear Regression

Results of regression analysis
Analysis Performed: Mon 18 Mar 2002 17:59:47
Data set used:
D:\Documents\Dbases\Analysis\DataFiles\ConsDLRBuy$
Rule set used:
D:\Documents\Dbases\Analysis\Rules\ConsDLRBuyRules

Dependent variable:	LInvest			
Total sum of squares	4.5430			
Regression sum of squares	3.4075			
Residual error	1.1355			
F-Statistic	34.7253			
Degrees of freedom	7,81			
R-squared	0.7501			

Variable	Coefficient	Standard Error	t-Statistic	Probability
Constant	0.0739			
C2	0.1448	0.0590	2.4559	0.0154
Crgo	−0.1246	0.0355	−3.5114	1.07E-03
FAge	−2.39E-03	1.71E-03	−1.3958	0.1631
Flyaway	−8.64E-04	1.54E-04	−5.6197	1.12E-05
FAge*Fly	2.33E-04	2.24E-05	10.4025	2.18E-08
Ramp5	1.1183	0.2344	4.7702	5.94E-05
FAge20^2	−3.19E-04	1.63E-04	−1.9592	0.0506

second-order term predicts the requirement for annual per-aircraft CLS expenditures as accurately as the second-order equation does, at least for the range of data available for this study. Therefore, we examined more closely the linear equation whose parameters are shown in Table 5.35.

First, we examined Cook's distance and leverage values in a scatterplot and we found that all data points were within acceptable levels for Cook's distance.

Practical Implications of the Reduced Equation

From the annual DLR modernization costs for a fighter costing $30 million and a cargo aircraft costing $100 million, in Figure 5.35,

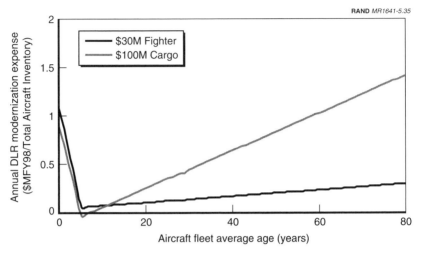

**Figure 5.35—DLR Purchases Experience a Sharp Initial Peak, Followed
by a Steady Growth as Fleets Age**

we can see that the DLR modernization costs experience an initial
peak, which diminishes rapidly over the first five years, then grows
steadily as the aircraft fleet ages further. Also obvious in the figure is
that more-expensive aircraft experience much higher growth.

How aircraft age affects the range of likely annual DLR purchases is
shown in Figure 5.36 for the $30-million aircraft and in Figure 5.37
for the $100-million aircraft. Fan-out is apparent at both older and
younger ages in these figures.

An Alternative Interpretation

The second-order deceleration term in Table 5.37 was very nearly
statistically significant. Figure 5.38 compares the forecasts from the
linear and second-order ("Decel") equations. If the second-order
equation were significant, it would forecast diminishing growth in
the demands for DLR modernization funds as fleets age. While the
demands might not fall as dramatically as the equation suggests at
the oldest ages, this study found some (almost statistically significant) evidence in the working capital fund data (USAF, 1994–1999)

that the demands for DLR modernization may moderate as fleets age beyond levels experienced to date.

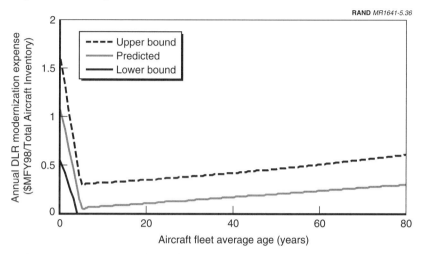

Figure 5.36— DLR Purchases for Less-Expensive Aircraft Fleets Are Less Certain at Both Young and Old Ages

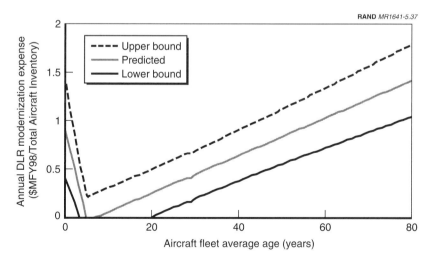

Figure 5.37—Uncertainties in DLR Purchases for More-Expensive Aircraft Fleets Increase at Very Young and Very Old Ages

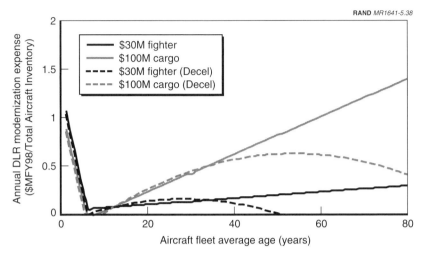

Figure 5.38—DLR Modernization Costs May Stabilize or Even Decline at Very High Ages

FINDINGS FOR TIME-CHANGE TECHNICAL ORDER (TCTO) DEPOT-LEVEL WORKLOADS

Table 5.38 shows the parameter-coefficient estimates for the full regression of TCTO depot-level workloads as aircraft fleets age. Although neither age-related term was statistically significant, the two 5-year break-in variables (Pulse5 and Ramp5) were significant, as were the flyaway cost and the bomber and tanker categorical variables.

A Stepwise Backward Regression Reduced the Independent Variables

We used a stepwise backward regression to eliminate the nonsignificant regression variables progressively, one at a time, until all coefficients had probabilities of .05 or less. Table 5.39 displays the final results from that process.

We can see that all the variables that were statistically significant in the initial full regression remained significant in the reduced equation. In addition, the helicopter (Helo) fleet categorical variables emerged as significant, along with the age-20-to-25 surge term (D20).

Table 5.38

Age Did Not Affect Annual Depot TCTO Workloads in the Full Regression

Results of regression analysis
Analysis Performed: Thu 5 Dec 2002 22:01:08
Data set used: D:\Documents\Dbases\Analysis\DataFiles\TCTO
Rule set used:
D:\Documents\Dbases\Analysis\Rules\TCTOMDCycleRules

Dependent variable:	LWork
Total sum of squares	1.6328E+10
Regression sum of squares	6.4892E+09
Residual error	9.8388E+09
F-Statistic	15.7558
Degrees of freedom	18,430
R-squared	0.3974

Variable	Coefficient	Standard Error	t-Statistic	Probability
Constant	173.3855			
Bmbr	3603.1214	1042.4217	3.4565	9.49E-04
C2	−178.1920	1032.8088	−0.1725	0.8574
Crgo	416.8533	762.4316	−0.5467	0.5917
Helo	1582.1018	884.3266	1.7890	0.0706
Tnkr	2336.1886	755.5066	3.0922	2.52E-03
Trnr	331.4423	890.8439	0.3721	0.7115
FAge	−61.8504	173.5685	0.3563	0.7224
D15	897.1004	1211.6040	0.7404	0.5338
D20	3084.0299	1982.6980	1.5555	0.1164
D25	656.9561	2788.0919	0.2356	0.8090
D30	2315.9843	3648.9310	0.6347	0.5332
D35	1299.4849	4633.6493	0.2804	0.7761
Flyaway	27.8739	2.5818	10.7962	3.19E-09
DAge*Fly	−0.3659	0.3589	−1.0196	0.3092
DPulse5	6640.7632	2015.0835	3.2955	1.46E-03
DPulse10	113.8246	1449.9373	0.0785	0.9354
DRamp5	−1.63E+04	3686.5412	−4.4226	8.23E-05
DRamp10	−1149.4220	4427.1970	−0.2596	0.7913

Table 5.39

Age Did Not Affect Annual Depot TCTO Workloads in the Reduced Regression

Results of regression analysis
Analysis Performed: Thu 05 Dec 2002 22:12:18
Data set used: D:\Documents\Dbases\Analysis\DataFiles\TCTO
Rule set used:
D:\Documents\Dbases\Analysis\Rules\TCTOMDCycleRules

Dependent variable:	LWork
Total sum of squares	1.6328E+10
Regression sum of squares	6.3701E+09
Residual error	9.9579E+09
F-Statistic	40.3012
Degrees of freedom	7,441
R-squared	0.3901

Variable	Coefficient	Standard Error	t-Statistic	Probability
Constant	-441.6292			
Bmbr	3263.5754	860.0802	3.7945	3.91E-04
Helo	1508.1571	722.6966	2.0867	0.0352
Tnkr	2099.3845	576.6574	3.6406	5.83E-04
D20	2153.3234	629.4613	3.4209	1.04E-03
Flyaway	26.1106	2.1154	12.3434	6.89E-10
Pulse5	6439.3980	1727.1245	3.7284	4.64E-04
Ramp5	−1.56E+04	2986.5330	−5.2137	1.37E-05

The Regression Detected No TCTO Workload Deceleration

As shown in Table 5.40, the regression found that the $FAge20^2$ factor was not significant beyond the .05 level when added to the reduced equation, so no significant level of second-order age-related growth occurs in TCTO workloads. Presumably, the equation without the second-order term predicts the requirement for annual TCTO workloads as accurately as does the second-order equation, at least for the range of data available for this study. Therefore, we examined more closely the linear equation whose parameters are shown in Table 5.39.

First, we examined Cook's distance and leverage values in a scatterplot, and we found that the four B-2A data points had Cook's distance values exceeding 1.0 and high leverage. A subsequent stepwise backward regression with those points removed found a different set of statistically significant factors. As shown in Table 5.41, the major differences in the equation without the B-2 data were that the 5-year pulse term and the helicopter fleet term were eliminated, the age–flyaway cost interaction became negative and significant, and the 5-year diminishing-ramp variable was reduced by almost 75 percent. The remaining significant factors had substantially different coefficients, changing the second, or even the first, decimal place.

Table 5.40

No Significant Deceleration Was Detected in the Reduced Regression of Annual Depot TCTO Workloads

Results of regression analysis
Analysis Performed: Thu 05 Dec 2002 22:14:00
Data set used: D:\Documents\Dbases\Analysis\DataFiles\TCTO
Rule set used:
D:\Documents\Dbases\Analysis\Rules\TCTOMDCycleRules

Dependent variable:	LWork			
Total sum of squares	1.6328E+10			
Regression sum of squares	6.3705E+09			
Residual error	9.9575E+09			
F-Statistic	35.1872			
Degrees of freedom	8,440			
R-squared	0.3902			

Variable	Coefficient	Standard Error	t-Statistic	Probability
Constant	−406.0173			
Bmbr	3299.9213	903.3465	3.6530	5.65E-04
Helo	1501.8513	725.0052	2..0715	0.0365
Tnkr	2112.4472	585.5919	3.6074	6.36E-04
D20	2165.1395	636.3925	3.4022	1.09E-03
Flyaway	26.0589	2.1531	12.1027	8.61E-10
DAge20^2	−0.0901	0.6773	−0.1330	0.8895
Pulse5	6406.3255	1746.8325	3.6674	5.44E-04
Ramp5	−1.56E+04	2989.9119	−5.2085	1.39E-05

Of course, during the 5-year period when the data were being collected, the B-2A had just been introduced to USAF operations. Therefore, its effects appear only in the first 5-year break-in period. Its unique design characteristics and breakthrough technologies for stealth may represent such a radical departure from previous capabilities and technologies that a new pattern for life-cycle modification workloads will emerge for future fleets based on that technology. Thus, its future TCTO workload pattern may not reflect the workload patterns that today's older fleets will experience.

That said, there is no fundamental reason to exclude the B-2A data from the analysis of depot TCTO workloads. If there had been some truly extraordinarily B-2A–unique event that caused the difference, or if there was some evidence that the data were erroneous, we might

Table 5.41

Removing B-2A Data Yielded a Simpler TCTO Workload Equation, in Which Age Was Statistically Significant

Results of regression analysis
Analysis Performed: Thu 05 Dec 2002 23:14:15
Data set used: D:\Documents\Dbases\Analysis\DataFiles\TCTO
Rule set used:
D:\Documents\Dbases\Analysis\Rules\TCTOMDCycleRules

Dependent variable:	LWork			
Total sum of squares	9.0698E+09			
Regression sum of squares	1.6785E+09			
Residual error	7.3913E+09			
F-Statistic	16.5395			
Degrees of freedom	6,437			
R-squared	0.1851			

Variable	Coefficient	Standard Error	t-Statistic	Probability
Constant	462.3583			
Bmbr	3430.8070	755.0136	4.5440	6.16E-05
Tnkr	1922.7833	489.8028	3.9256	2.80E-04
D20	2554.5135	555.7328	4.5967	5.44E-05
Flyaway	29.1850	5.1095	5.7119	4.91E-06
DAge*Fly	–1.0121	0.3145	–3.2181	1.79E-03
Ramp5	–4839.7648	1543.0887	–3.1364	2.23E-03

wish to remove the data. As it is, the mere fact that its initial TCTO workloads differ strongly from the workloads of other aircraft platforms during the same time is not sufficient reason to exclude its data from this analysis.

Practical Implications of the Reduced Equations

Figure 5.39 shows the annual depot and contractor workloads in hours per aircraft for a fighter costing $30 million and a cargo aircraft costing $100 million. As we can see in the figure, the TCTO workload experiences a brief initial peak about age 5. After that, the workload stabilizes at a level that depends on the aircraft flyaway cost, except or a surge in the 5-year period after the aircraft design has been fielded 20 years.

How aircraft age affects the range of likely TCTO workloads is shown in Figure 5.40 for the $30-million fighter and in Figure 5.41 for the $100-million cargo aircraft. Age is not a variable in the regression equation, so we cannot observe any fan-out as either fleet ages.

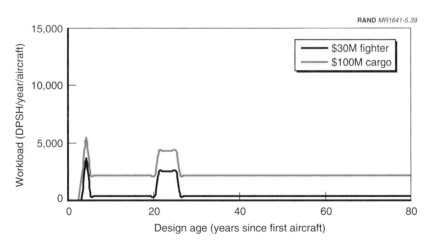

Figure 5.39—TCTO Workloads Stabilize After an Initial Unstable Period, Then Surge at the Start of the Third Decade of Operations

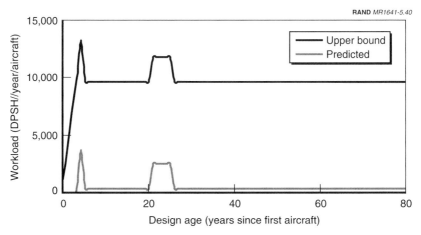

Figure 5.40—Fighters' TCTO Workload Uncertainties Do Not Vary with Aircraft Age

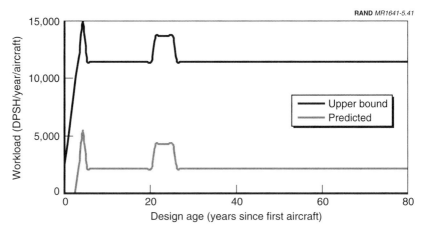

Figure 5.41—Cargo Aircraft TCTO Workload Uncertainties Do Not Vary with Aircraft Age

However, we are struck by the very large range of probable outcomes, where that range exceeds the expected TCTO workload by many times.

An Alternative Interpretation

As mentioned above, eliminating the B-2A from the regression analysis yields a substantially different equation. Figure 5.42 displays the forecasts for the $100-million cargo aircraft based on the regression analysis without the B-2A data. The alternative analysis suggests that the TCTO workloads may reach a lower initial peak, then decline slowly over the remainder of the aircraft's life cycle, with the exception of the 5-year surge after the aircraft has been fielded 20 years.

While the steadily declining workload is an important difference between the two analyses, the analyses share three important similarities. Both display an initially low 5-year break-in period, and both show a surge in the period when the design age is between 20 and 25 years. Finally, both show a higher TCTO workload overall for more-expensive aircraft.

SUMMARY OF MAJOR AGE-RELATED FINDINGS

Table 5.42 displays the significant relationships we found between age and late-life workload and material consumption. Of the 13

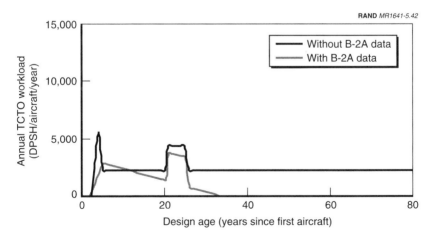

Figure 5.42—TCTO Workloads May Decline as Fleets Age

maintenance and modification workload and material consumption categories, 11 exhibit patterns of late-life growth. The exceptions are base periodic inspections and TCTOs.

Of the categories exhibiting growth, only one—special inspections—exhibited the same rate of growth for all aircraft. All other growing categories exhibited a positive relationship between the aircraft fly-away cost (or engine weight) and the rate of late-life workload or material consumption growth, the more-expensive aircraft (and heavier engines) workloads growing faster with age than less-expensive (or lighter) ones.

Only one category—GSD material consumption—showed a statistically significant sign of abating growth rates with aircraft age. The negative second-order effect for this category tended to reduce the growth of GSD consumption to near-zero levels near the end of the currently available data.

The most troubling finding was that PDM workloads appear to accelerate as fleets enter their second and third decades of operation. Although we found no evidence that other workloads grow at anything other than a linear rate, PDM workloads in this study exhibited pronounced higher rates of growth after age 20 years.

Some Uncertainties Remain

Many factors other than age affect workloads and material consumption. This study was able to control only some of those factors statistically. Estimates of the 95-percent confidence intervals for the two notional aircraft indicate that some workloads can be predicted more accurately than others, assuming the equations are correct. We also found evidence that supports alternative age-related growth patterns for a few workloads, as shown in Table 5.43.

First, engineers familiar with one older fleet (KC-135 ESL Integrated Product Team, 2000) suggest that fleets' PDM workload growth will moderate over the next few years as some one-time repairs are finished and inspection workloads reach their natural limits. That future transition cannot be detected in any analysis of recent historical

Table 5.42

Primary Study Results: Significant Age-Related Growth Rates

Name	Units	Base Growth Rate	Cost/ Weight Sensitivity	Second-Order Factor	Regression Table
On-Equipment Workload	MMH/ aircraft FH	n.s.[a]	0.0067/ $M-year	n.s.	5.2
Off-Equipment Workload	MMH/ aircraft FH	n.s.	0.00201/ $M-year	n.s.	5.5
Base Periodic Inspection Workload	MMH/ aircraft FH	n.s.	n.s.	n.s.	5.8
Special Inspection Workload	MMH/ aircraft FH	.0321/ year	n.s.	n.s.	5.11
DLR Repair Cost	$(FY98)/ aircraft FH	n.s.	0.6626/ $M-year	n.s.	5.14
GSD Material Cost	$/aircraft FH	n.s.	0.0846/ $M-year	−0.3221/ (year −20)^2	5.18
Replacement Equipment	$(FY98)/ PAA	−880/ year	32.19/ $M-year	n.s.	5.20
Programmed Depot Maintenance Workload	DPSH/ PDM	301/ year	8.57/ $M-year	26.26/ (year −20)^2	5.24
Engine Overhaul	DPSH/ engine FH	n.s.	.0000162/ lb-year	n.s.	5.26
CLS Costs (per Aircraft)	$(FY98)/ aircraft	n.s.	1,693/ $M-year	n.s.	5.29
CLS Costs (per FH)	$(FY98)/ FH	n.s.	0.2282/ $M-year	n.s.	5.32
Depot-Level Reparable Purchases	$FY98/ TAI	−0.0037/ year	0.000231/ $M-year	n.s.	5.36
Depot Time Change Technical Order Workloads	DPSH/ TAI	n.s.	n.s.	n.s.	5.39

[a]n.s. indicates a nonsignificant relationship.

data. If the second-order growth found in this study was caused by a systematic pattern in which inspections increase to new higher but stable levels in late life and some one-time workloads emerge, the PDM workload acceleration may be misleading. The first row in Table 5.43 indicates the PDM growth if the acceleration term is removed from the regression.

The second row in that table suggests that the per-flying-hour growth in CLS expenses may be much larger. That result arose from a regression analysis that was performed because a statistical test indicated that the E-9A data may have unduly influenced the basic results. If so, comparing the growth rates in the two tables, we see that the growth rate might be over 40 percent higher than indicated in the basic equation.

A more intriguing finding arose in the TCTO analysis from a similar test, which indicated B-2A data may have unduly influenced the basic results. With the B-2A data removed, we found a *negative* relationship between age and TCTO workloads. If the underlying rela-

Table 5.43

Alternative Age-Related Growth Rates

Name	Reason for Alternative	Units	Base Growth Rate	Cost/ Weight Sensi- tivity	Second- Order Factor	Regression Table
Programmed Depot Mainte- nance Workload	Late-life emergence of PDM workload growth	DPSH/ PDM	487 per year	7.47/ $M-year	Excluded	5.23
CLS Costs (per FH)	E-9A data excluded	$FY98/ FH	n.s.[a]	0.3257/ $M-year	n.s.	5.34
Depot Time Change Technical Order Work- loads	B-2A data excluded	DPSH/ TAI	n.s.	−1.0121/ $M-year	n.s.	5.41

[a]n.s. indicates a nonsignificant relationship.

tionship is negative, modification workloads may diminish for older aircraft, except for a periodic major upgrade every 20-odd years as the service recommits itself to relying on that aging platform for an extended period.

Chapter Six

IMPLICATIONS

The findings discussed in Chapter Five present the U.S. Air Force with several profound and difficult choices about its future aircraft fleets. The choices are profound because, once made, they will set the course for developing and maintaining the Air Force's military capabilities over the next two or three decades. They are difficult because so little is certain about either the demands for those capabilities or the Air Force acquisition and maintenance system's ability to supply them.

One thing is certain. If the Air Force retains its aging fleets as planned and if those fleets' maintenance workloads and material consumption continue to grow with fleet ages according to the patterns reported in Chapter Five, annual maintenance costs will increase and the number of aircraft available for operations and training will decrease. (An analysis using these findings is in progress to estimate both cost and availability consequences for the current force-structure plan.)

SIX STRATEGIES

Broadly, the service can follow any of six broad strategies to manage its aircraft fleets' capabilities over the next 20 or so years:

1. Continue the current plan.

2. Replace fleets sooner.

3. Reduce force size.

4. Accelerate modification initiatives.

5. Increase maintenance capacity.

6. Streamline and modernize maintenance.

The current USAF force-structure strategy calls for maintaining approximately today's force structure over the next 20 or so years: replacing aging fighters and some cargo aircraft and starting to replace tankers.   Strategy 2 would accelerate that process, retiring older fleets earlier, although at some substantial cost. Strategy 3 reduces force size, thereby making additional funds available for buying replacement fleets.   Strategy 4 would modify the existing fleets in ways that would reduce future maintenance workloads and costs, although at some interim investment cost and availability loss. Strategy 5 would invest in improved maintenance capacity, preserving or improving aircraft availability as workloads grow, but at some additional expense. Finally, Strategy 6 would enhance both the processes and the technology associated with maintenance, reducing maintenance flow times and minimizing annual expenses, although at the expense of additional initial investments.

No single strategy will be sufficient. Indeed, the Air Force already has initiatives under way to modify the existing force structure and maintenance plans, employing all these broad strategies except the third. For example, efforts are under way to:

- Replace portions of the tanker fleet earlier.

- Implement major structural upgrades for the F-16C fleet and improve C-5 fleet departure reliability.

- Invest in additional facilities and equipment to modernize and expand the Air Logistics Centers.

- Introduce more-responsive producer-supplier processes and acquire improved nondestructive inspection technologies.

These initiatives and related efforts will almost certainly help the Air Force reduce future maintenance workloads or increase its ability to absorb those workloads.

Unfortunately, the Air Force has little ability to estimate how much a particular initiative may contribute to the future availability and costs of individual fleets, let alone to compare multiple alternative initiatives or assess how those initiatives would affect how much military capability each fleet can contribute over time. In the past, it has not been possible to forecast costs and availabilities for alternative force structures and maintenance or modification investment plans to see how current investment choices may affect future military capabilities.

This research provides the foundation for such forecasts and assessments of applying alternative force structure and maintenance strategies to individual fleets and to the Air Force as a whole. These workload forecasts can be used with maintenance-capacity plans to forecast such operational measures as maintenance (or modification) flow times and available aircraft for different maintenance capacities; the costs can be computed directly from the maintenance capacity and the associated resource requirements. Then, it will be possible to develop trade-offs among the six strategies, and even trade-offs across the various fleets contributing to a given military capability.

FACING DEMAND AND SUPPLY UNCERTAINTIES

If we were omniscient and could see the future clearly, those assessments of alternative strategies for each fleet would be enough. We could assess each alternative, then pick the alternative with the best fleet availability and cost.

Unfortunately, nobody knows precisely how much of any military capability will be required in the future; even more unfortunately, nobody knows for sure what new maintenance requirements will emerge as today's fleets continue to age. The USAF might encounter both demand surprises—for example, a capability mix other than the one planned is required—and supply surprises—for example, the forecast maintenance workloads and material requirements suddenly diverge from those planned. The focus in this study is on the latter type of surprises: whether the maintenance establishment can deliver the required aircraft availability and modernization schedule at an acceptable cost.

A close reading of Chapter Five should leave some doubts about the size of future workloads. First, every workload regression has unexplained variance: errors between the actual data and the regression forecast—*assuming the equations are basically correct.* In some cases (off-equipment workloads, base periodic inspections, DLR repair, depot-level TCTOs), the forecast errors are so large that the 95-percent confidence lower bound is negative. In other cases (special inspections, GSD consumption, PDMs, per-flying-hour CLS costs), the variability grows rapidly with forecasts beyond current experience. The Air Force needs to be prepared for some wide variations in requirements for specific workload or material categories for individual fleets over time.

Fortunately, the central limit theorem in probability theory suggests that those variations may substantially cancel each other out in the aggregate for the entire force. But such cancellation is not guaranteed. The theorem assumes that the errors are independent, which may not be the case. So long as it is the case, the current management practice of redirecting funds across programs should mitigate the more drastic effects of those statistical demand variations.

The more troubling uncertainties are the nonstatistical ones for which any probability based on historical evidence cannot be measured. For example, Chapter Three makes the case for an eventual limit to the growth of metal-structure inspection and repair workloads associated with PDMs. Yet, the statistical analysis in Chapter Five found no such limit within current fleets' service lives. Almost certainly, some limit exists. But we cannot be certain, yet, about when the PDM workload limit will emerge.

It may never emerge. New material-deterioration processes may appear that simply add to the PDM workload. In the past two decades, corrosion and wiring deterioration have been recognized as common problems affecting older aircraft. More recently, engineers have begun to raise concerns about the potential service life of composite materials. It is entirely possible that the workload-limit hypothesis is correct for a single workload such as metal-structure inspection and repair; however, new workloads may continue to emerge as fleets age.

Likewise, the Air Force should not assume that only PDM workloads have uncertain futures that cannot be characterized statistically.

Other workloads, particularly modifications to meet emerging operational challenges, may also grow in unpredictable ways.

We might not be too concerned about those uncertainties if it were not for their effects on future workloads and fielded military capabilities. If a critical maintenance requirement emerges that grounds or restricts the operations of a fleet, the maintenance estab-lishment's ability to restore that fleet to full operational capability will limit the availability of that fleet for operations and training. That same ability is key to modifying a fleet to meet new operational requirements while maintaining acceptable aircraft availability.

Three basic strategies must be managed in the face of uncertainty: get more information, build a contingency plan, and hedge. The Air Force needs to pursue all three for its aging fleets.

First, it must seek more information about the maintenance chal-lenges facing its fleets, both in general and for specific fleets. Although scientific and engineering models exist for metal-structure fatigue, research on the deterioration and maintenance processes for wiring, composite damage, and corrosion is still at a primitive level. More important, even the challenges of structural fatigue facing individual fleets often reach near-critical stages before they receive sufficient attention to warrant funding for remedial action. The Air Force needs to develop a comprehensive fleet-assessment method-ology that informs planners and senior officers well in advance about all the emerging challenges and maintenance needs and their impli-cations for flight safety, availability, and cost. Such a methodology is being addressed by Project AIR FORCE in a project for the Aircraft Enterprise office in Aeronautical Systems Command (ASC/AA).

Second, the Air Force needs to build contingency plans, such as those suggested by Greenfield and Persselin (2002). Wrestling with the issue of when it is most cost-efficient to replace an aircraft fleet, they addressed the inherent uncertainties about how future work-loads and costs would evolve. They then suggested the notion of a *trigger point,* a level that, once exceeded by workloads, would still leave enough time for the Air Force to acquire a replacement fleet before the costs got out of hand. Ideally, such plans would be devel-oped in advance so that they could be executed quickly, thereby minimizing the undesirable consequences if the costs were rising too rapidly. Greenfield and Persselin's work is being extended in Project AIR FORCE to make the trade-off more responsive to changes in aircraft availability.

Third, the Air Force needs to hedge against the possibility that an individual fleet may have a cost or availability surprise. Dewar et al. (1993) suggest that shaping actions can be taken to avoid surprises by identifying critical assumptions and taking action to avert the failure of those assumptions. This strategy applies to both old and young fleets, because newly designed and fielded fleets are prone to design and manufacturing defects that may have been missed in initial operational testing and evaluation. One shaping action might be to acquire multiple fleets capable of each mission, so the Air Force will be less susceptible to any turbulence in an individual fleet's cost or availability. Of course, such a hedging strategy is more expensive than a strategy optimized for an optimistic set of assumptions, but it reduces susceptibility to surprises.

Again, the findings reported in Chapter Five should aid in this strategy process. By evaluating costs and availabilities in scenarios in which the uncertainties identified in Chapter Five are considered in addition to the main findings, Air Force planners should be able to test the robustness of alternative investment plans for force structure and maintenance.

Adams, John L., John B. Abell, and Karen Isaacson, *Modeling and Forecasting the Demand for Aircraft Recoverable Spare Parts,* Santa Monica, Calif.: RAND, R-4211/AF/OSD, 1993.

Athearn, Capt (USAF) Chris, Doug Black, and Tony Chutek, *Engine Life Management Plan for the F100-PW-229,* Wright-Patterson AFB, Ohio: Aeronautical Systems Command, 30 September 1998.

Boeing Corporation, 2001 Aircraft Prices, www.boeing.com/commercial/prices/index.html, 3 August 2001.

Camm, Frank A., and H. L. Shulman, *When Internal Transfer Prices and Costs Differ: How Stock Funding of Depot-Level Reparables Affects Decision Making in the Air Force,* Santa Monica, Calif.: RAND, MR-307-AF, 1993.

Crawford, Gordon B., *Variability in the Demands for Aircraft Spare Parts: Its Magnitude and Implications,* Santa Monica, Calif.: RAND, R-3318-AF, 1988.

Dewar, James A., Carl H. Builder, William M. Hix, and Morlie H. Levin, *Assumption-Based Planning: A Planning Tool for Very Uncertain Times,* Santa Monica, Calif.: RAND, MR-114-A, 1993.

DiDonato, Michael, and Gregory Sweers, *The Economic Considerations of Operating Post Production Aircraft Beyond Design Service Objectives,* Seattle, Wash.: Boeing, 4 December 1997.

"Fixed-Wing Aircraft Trends," *Aerospace Daily,* January 31, 2001, p. 168.

Francis, Peter, and Geoff Shaw, "Effect of Aircraft Age on Maintenance Costs," briefing, Center for Naval Analyses (CNA), Alexandria, Va., 2000.

Gansler, Jacques, Statement to Defense Science Board, quoted in Zoellick, Robert B., "Statement to the Committee on the Budget of the U.S. Senate," Washington, D.C.: Center for Strategic and International Studies, 24 February 1999.

Goure, Daniel, and Jeffrey M. Ranney, *Averting the Defense Train Wreck in the New Millennium,* Significant Issues Series, Vol. XXI, No. 6, Washington, D.C.: Center for Strategic and International Studies, November 1999.

Greenfield, Victoria A., and David Persselin, *An Economic Framework for Evaluating Military Aircraft Replacement,* Santa Monica, Calif.: RAND, MR-1489-AF, 2002.

Hildebrandt, Gregory G., and Man-Bing Sze, *An Estimation of USAF Aircraft Operating and Support Cost Relations,* Santa Monica, Calif.: RAND, N-3062-ACQ, May 1990.

Holmes, Oliver Wendell, "The Deacon's Masterpiece," 1858, in http://www.slickninja.com/archives/shay.html, 3 August 2001.

Johnson, John A., *Age Impacts on Operating and Support Costs; Navy Aircraft Age Analysis Methodology,* Pautuxent River, Md.: Naval Aviation and Maintenance Office (NAMO), August 1993.

Johnson, R. E., *Forecasting the Maintenance Manpower Needs of the Depot System,* Santa Monica, Calif.: RAND, RM-3163-PR, June 1962.

KC-135 ESL Integrated Product Team, *KC-135 Economic Service Life Study,* Tinker AFB, Okla.: Boeing, Technical Report EA 00-023R2-135OTH, 2001.

Kiley, Gregory T., *The Effects of Aging on the Costs of Maintaining Military Equipment,* Washington, D.C.: Congressional Budget Office, August 2001.

Marks, Kenneth E., and Ronald W. Hess, *Estimating Aircraft Depot Maintenance Costs,* Santa Monica, Calif.: RAND, R-2731-PA&E, July 1981.

Mehuron, Tamar A., "Budgets," in *Air Force Almanac, Air Force Magazine,* and *Air Force Association,* May issues, 1992–2001.

Nelson, J. R., *Life Cycle Analysis of Aircraft Turbine Engines,* Santa Monica, Calif.: RAND, R-2103-AF, 1977.

Office of the Secretary of Defense (OSD), Cost Analysis Improvement Group (CAIG), "Aircraft Operating and Support Cost Element Structure Definitions," in *Operating and Support Cost Estimating Guide,* Appendix C, Washington, D.C., May 1992.

Paulson, Robert M., and Karl Hoffmayer, "Mobilization and Wartime Depot Aircraft Repair Workloads," Santa Monica, Calif.: unpublished RAND research, March 1980.

Pratt & Whitney, *F-117-PW-100 Engine Structural Integrity Program (ENSIP) Engine Life Management Plan (ELMP),* West Palm Beach, Fla., 30 September 1998.

Pyles, Raymond, and Hyman L. Shulman, *United States Air Force Fighter Support in Operation Desert Storm,* Santa Monica, Calif.: RAND, MR-468-AF, 1995.

Ramsey, Thomas, Carl French, and Kenneth R. Sperry, "Airframe Maintenance Trend Analysis," briefing, Oklahoma City Air Logistics Center, Tinker AFB, Okla., 1998.

Ratliff, Kyle J., and LCDR David C. Tiller, "CNO Flying Hour Program: Naval Center for Cost Analysis Model," briefing to SCEA Conference, Naval Center for Cost Analysis, Washington, D.C., June 1999.

Roche, James, quoted in "Roche Growing Increasingly Concerned About Aging Aircraft," *Inside the Air Force,* 24 May 2002.

Ryan, Gen Michael E., quoted in "Air Force Chief of Staff Cites Readiness Concerns," *Air Force News,* 27 October 1999.

Sperry, Kenneth, *KC-135 Cost of Ownership,* Oklahoma City, Okla.: Boeing, July 1998.

Stoll, Laurence, and Stan Davis, *Aircraft Age Impact on Individual Operating and Support Cost Elements,* Pautuxent River, Md.: NAMO, July 1993.

U.S. Air Force, *1999 Air Force Weighted Inflation Indices,* Washington, D.C.: SAF/FMC, Air Force Instruction 65-503, Table A49-1, at http://www.saffm.hq.af.mil, December 1998.

U.S. Air Force, *Depot Maintenance of Aerospace Vehicles and Training Equipment,* Air Force Tasking Order (AFTO) 00-25-4, 31 May 1999.

U.S. Air Force, "F110 Program Management Review," briefing slides, Oklahoma City Air Logistics Center, Tinker AFB, Okla., 29 June 1998.

U.S. Air Force, *FY2001 Amended Budget Request, Air Force Aircraft Procurement,* Volume 1, *Committee Staff Procurement Backup Book,* Washington, D.C.: SAF/FMB, February 2000.

U.S. Air Force, *United States Air Force Working Capital Fund, Fiscal Year Budget Estimates,* Washington, D.C., 1994–1999.

U.S. Air Force, Air Force Cost Analysis Improvement Group (AFCAIG), *A2-1 Logistics Cost Factors BY01,* Washington, D.C.: Air Force Instruction 65-503, Attachment 2-1, December 2000a.

U.S. Air Force, AFCAIG, *A6-1 Contractor Logistics Support (CLS) Cost Factors BY01,* Washington, D.C.: Air Force Instruction 65-503, Attachment 6-1, June 2000b.

U.S. Air Force, AFCAIG, *A6-1 Contractor Logistics Support (CLS) Cost Factors BY99,* Washington, D.C.: Air Force Instruction 65-503, Attachment 6-1, December 1998a.

U.S. Air Force, Air Force Cost Analysis Improvement Group (AFCAIG), *FY99 Logistics Factors,* Air Force Instruction 65-503, Attachment 2-1, December 1998b.

U.S. Air Force, AFCAIG, *Unit Flyaway Costs,* Washington, D.C.: Air Force Instruction 65-503, Table A10-1, http://www.saffm.hq.af.mil, 12 May 1998c.

U.S. Air Force, Oklahoma City Air Logistics Center, *Engine Life Management Plan for F-16C/D/F110-GE-100/Block 30/40*, Version 8, Tinker AFB, Okla., 13 February 1998.

U.S. Air Force, San Antonio Air Logistics Center (SA-ALC), *Engine Handbook*, spreadsheet, Kelly AFB, Texas, 1999a.

U.S. Air Force, SA-ALC, *FY99/00 Engine Overhaul Depot Product Standard Hours*, Spreadsheet, Kelly AFB, Texas: SA-ALC Engine Program Management Office, 1999b.